HIDDEN INHERITANCE

FAMILY SECRETS, MEMORY, AND FAITH

HEIDI B. NEUMARK

For now we see through a glass, darkly;
but then face to face: now I know in part;
but then shall I know even as also I am known.

1 Corinthians 13:12 KJV

ABINGDON PRESS
NASHVILLE

HIDDEN INHERITANCE
FAMILY SECRETS, MEMORY, AND FAITH

Copyright © 2015 by Heidi B. Neumark

Library of Congress Cataloging-in-Publication Data

Neumark, Heidi.
  Hidden inheritance : family secrets, memory, and faith / Heidi B. Neumark.— First [edition].
    1 online resource.
  Includes bibliographical references.
  Description based on print version record and CIP data provided by publisher; resource not viewed.
  ISBN 978-1-63088-125-2 (e-pub)—ISBN 978-1-63088-124-5 (binding: pbk.)
  1. Neumark, Heidi. 2. Lutheran Church—Clergy—Biography. 3. Women clergy— United States—Biography. 4. Holocaust, Jewish (1939-1945)—Influence. I. Title.
  BX8080.N463

284.1092—dc23

15 16 17 18 19 20 21 22 23 24—10 9 8 7 6 5 4 3 2 1

MANUFACTURED IN THE UNITED STATES OF AMERICA

Praise for *Hidden Inheritance*

"Faced suddenly, and quite unexpectedly, with her family's history of horror, Heidi Neumark has written a memoir that is by turns intimate, spelling-binding, and revelatory. Born of personal desperation, her story carries us through the blistered soul of modernity to the recollection that is redemption. It moves me to even talk about this courageous, beautiful book!"
—Charles Marsh, author of *Strange Glory: A Life of Dietrich Bonhoeffer*

"In this memoir, Heidi Neumark once again demonstrates her mastery of the genre, this time taking the reader on a personal pilgrimage through Nazi Germany, the Holocaust, and her own newly discovered Jewish identity. *Hidden Inheritance* is part detective story, part memoir, but most of all an exquisite meditation on the fractured family of Christians and Jews as seen by one who now lives in both worlds. There is much to be learned from her story, much to be repented, and much to be felt. A book not only to be read but absorbed."
—Richard Lischer, Duke Divinity School, author of *Stations of the Heart: Parting with a Son*

"I have been waiting impatiently for the next book from Heidi Neumark because she is my favorite chronicler of the craziness of Christian life, but *Hidden Inheritance* is so much more. It sweeps you up like kin for a wild reunion with ancestors you will want to know better. From her unexpected discovery of Jewish ancestry, to the eclectic mix at her New York church, to the odd company of Lutheran clergy and eccentric everyday family life, Neumark's story evokes the mighty cloud of witnesses that ultimately connects us all. This is a family tree worth climbing."
—Lillian Daniel, author of *When "Spiritual But Not Religious" Is Not Enough* and *This Odd and Wondrous Calling*

"In her thirty years as a Lutheran pastor, Heidi Neumark had listened to many secrets. In *Hidden Inheritance* she pursues a

surprising secret in her own family: her late father's Jewish lineage. Her gracefully written and evocative memoir narrates her journey to trace the lives of her Jewish ancestors, many of whom lost their lives in the Shoah. Her book is enthralling reading, not simply for the drama of her search for Jewish family members, but also for her sensitive reflections on her own inner journey and the connections with her congregants."
—Dr. Mary C. Boys, Dean of Academic Affairs, Skinner and McAlpin Professor of Practical Theology, Union Theological Seminary

"I couldn't put this book down. Rev. Neumark takes us on a compelling journey through multi-generations of a single family and through multi-layers of history. With courage and compassion Neumark raises complex questions of identity and theology. This is a book for Christians and Jews and for all who live with family secrets and for all who struggle with the paradox of deriving life from a tradition that robbed others of life. Ultimately this is an inspiring and beautifully told true story of death and rebirth."
—Rabbi Margaret Moers Wenig, D.D., President-elect of the Academy of Homiletics, Instructor in Liturgy and Homiletics, Hebrew Union College-Jewish Institute of Religion, NY

"Any person of any faith would be moved to read this extraordinary account of faith drawn from an awareness of true evil. From coerced assimilation in Lübeck to the concentration camps, from a Lutheran parish in the South Bronx to a Passover seder in Southern California, Rev. Neumark relates her spiritual reflections upon the Nazi evil that effaced the Jewishness of her ancestors, tortured them, and ultimately murdered her grandfather, even as it pointed her family toward the Christianity that brings her joy and salvation. May the memories of Moritz, Ida, and Hans Neumark be a blessing."
—Rabbi Jeremy Kalmanofsky, Congregation Ansche Chesed, New York City

"For Zion's sake I will not keep silent."
Isaiah 62:1a NRSV

Kurt Neumark—Izbica
Paula Neumark—Izbica
Julius Neumark—Theresienstadt
Paul Neumark—Auschwitz
Willi Neumark—Berlin
Edgar Neumark—Brandenburg
Richard Neumark—Brandenburg
Karl Heinz Neumark—Brandenburg
George Neumark—Minsk
Anna Neumark—Minsk
Richard Neumark— Auschwitz
Joanna Neumark—Auschwitz
Hans Neumark—Auschwitz
Ernst Neumark—Dresden
Walter Neumark—Izbica

And especially
Moritz Neumark—Theresienstadt
Ida Neumark
Hans R. Neumark

This is for you.

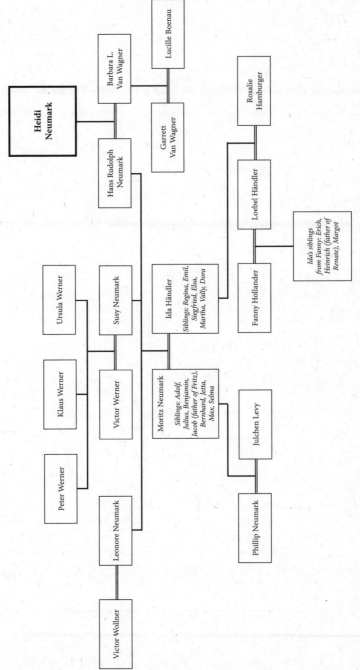

Contents

Contents

PREFACE: GOOGLING MOSES

. . . the shadows of time lie like questions Over our secret.
—Nelly Sachs

There is nothing unusual about the crowd of shoppers waiting in line at Park East Kosher in Manhattan's Yorkville neighborhood. It's Friday morning, and they are here to buy top-quality brisket, shanks of lamb, stuffed cabbage, chicken, and rib steak ready for take-out. Together we breathe in the warm scent of braided challah set out in gleaming rows on metal carts. Everyone in the deli is Jewish except for me, blinking back sudden tears. I am in the neighborhood and have stopped by the store for a sandwich, never expecting a surge of sorrow along with my liverwurst on rye. I am surrounded by Jews preparing for the Sabbath, and I long to be part of them, which makes no sense, since I am a Lutheran pastor.

Two years earlier, just after midnight, the ringing cell phone beside my bed woke me up with a rush of adrenalin. I wondered who had died. Did I need to put on my clerics and head to a hospital? But no, this was my daughter, Ana, calling with news that I am still trying to absorb. Did I know that I was Jewish? Did I know that my grandfather died in a concentration camp? Did I know that my grandmother was a death-camp survivor? What I knew is that my grandfather Moritz died of a heart attack before I was born. This is what my father told me when I asked what had happened to Opa. I knew my parents were lifelong Lutherans, and I'd served as a Lutheran pastor for nearly thirty years. We were a Christian family so when Ana said that her information came from Wikipedia, I almost laughed. This was clearly a case of mistaken identity, or identities oddly conjoined in cyberspace.

Sunday morning and multiple church services were fast approaching. I needed to sleep, but instead I got up and went downstairs to find Ana sitting in bed with the computer propped on her lap. She was twenty-two and living at home while finishing grad school for early-childhood special education. Ana had been up late Googling family names, and when she hit on Moritz Neumark, a page opened the door into an alternate reality where Moritz had morphed into a child named Moses Lazarus. I was sucked into a vortex of revelations as one website pulled me into another and then another, imploding the old verities of my life.

Hours later, while it was still dark, I fell back into bed, grateful for my husband, Gregorio, who reached to grasp my hand, sleepily unaware that I was not the person I thought I was. I lay wide-eyed on the sheets, disoriented and wrapped in sadness. How was it possible that I was never told the truth? I believed that I was especially close to my parents, their only child. I believed that they had passed their faith on to me as they had inherited it from their own parents and their parents before them. My maternal grandparents met and fell in love as teenagers in a Lutheran youth group at their Brooklyn church. Admittedly I was less clear about the courtship of my father's parents, but they had raised my father and his two sisters as German Lutherans, or so I thought.

I knew that my father came to the United States from Germany in 1938. He had earned a doctorate in chemical engineering and begun his career at the iron works plant built and directed by his father. A few years later, his parents put him on a boat headed for New York in order to give him a better, more stable future than seemed possible in Germany at the time. This made sense to me and was true, as far as it went, which turns out not to have been very far at all. What I hadn't known was that soon after my father landed here, my Jewish grandparents were deported to Theresienstadt (Terezín), a concentration camp in what is now the Czech Republic. My grandmother survived. My grandfather did not.

* * *

At 6:30 the alarm goes off and I make myself get up. I follow my usual Sunday morning routine. . . . take shower, get dressed, drink coffee, pray. I've been doing this for thirty years—nineteen of them in the South Bronx and another decade here at Trinity Lutheran Church of Manhattan, but this Sunday is different. I take the shower and button up my black clergy shirt and drink the coffee, but I can't pray. I can't focus on the task before me. My mind is somewhere else.

What does it mean that my faith has come to me not as I imagined—a cherished inheritance handed down from generation to generation—but through a trail of terror? As someone committed to interfaith understanding, I am conscious of the ongoing challenges to the survival of the Jewish people. Now it appears that within my own family there was a break in the chain of generations of Jews. Even worse is realizing that the rupture occurred because of what I can only understand as evil. I feel something akin to seasickness in my mind and gut, aching for solid ground that had dissolved. But I have to pull myself together and show up at church.

Like my congregation in the Bronx, Trinity is a multi-ethnic community with a strong social-justice orientation. Both churches welcome new immigrants and their children, mostly from south of our border, so I will be leading worship in Spanish as well as in English. When I arrive, Emilio is making coffee and setting out juice for the snack time that happens after the earliest service of the day. We call it Wee Worship because it's focused on the special gifts and needs of very young children and I will preach with puppets. Ten years ago, Emilio was a student in the first confirmation class I taught at this church and now he lives here at Trinity Place, our shelter for homeless LGBTQ youth. The residents have put their beds away, and Emilio is transforming the room for Sunday School and coffee hour. Tomorrow the same hall will host restaurant delivery workers meeting with a labor organizer, a prayer group, and an afterschool program for children.

For me, the strands of worship, community organizing, advocacy, and solidarity with those who are marginalized and oppressed have always been intertwined. Now I wonder if my life's calling has been shaped by the hidden pull of family history. Jews mark the end of the Sabbath with a ceremony that includes a braided candle with multiple wicks burning into a single flame. The braiding is a reminder of unity and harmony at the conclusion of the Sabbath. It reminds me of the interweaving in my work and now between my past and my present.

As the little ones run up the stairs for Wee Worship, I realize that I am not the only one in church this morning who is haunted by questions and longing to know more about my roots. A number of the children poking around in the basket of instruments have never known their father. A preschooler clinging to her mother is adopted from the other side of the world where her birth mother left her carefully wrapped in a purple quilt on the side of the road. Three rambunctious little boys come in with their father who is fine with them calling her dad even though she is now a woman. I am hardly alone in wresting with issues of identity.

Throughout the morning, I will look out on people of all ages filled with their own questions over things left unsaid and unexplained, aching to know more. As a pastor, I'm very aware of the secrets people carry around and the relief that can come from speaking the unspeakable. Most things get silenced in families because of shame, guilt, and fear. People wonder what possible good can come from bringing up a painful or shameful past. Like, the mother who wonders if she should tell one daughter that her sister was molested by a cousin for years? It will only be upsetting and split the family apart. Yet so much can be lost in an effort to protect others from censure or embarrassment, and fissures under the surface tend to emerge one way or another. I can't answer for everyone, but I've seen how ongoing silence itself can cause tremendous pain—and how it can be crazy-making. It's possible to cover something up, but we can't unsee, unknow, or unfeel it and remain whole. Ironically, I never realized that this was true in my own family. Now, I've joined the club.

CHAPTER ONE

CROSSING OVER

My German Trousseau

When I was little, I begged both of my parents for stories from their own childhoods. I knew that my father grew up with servants, which seemed very exotic, and I wanted to hear all about it. I knew that on laundry day, the cook did not have time to prepare a regular meal but always made *Rote Grütze*, a red currant pudding my father loved. When I was a teenager, I learned to make this dish when my father lost his appetite before being diagnosed with colon cancer. I became a *Rote Grütze* expert and prepared the dish with vanilla sauce to tempt him to eat.

The cook's husband served as the chauffeur, and there was also a groundskeeper and a governess. I knew the garden was large enough for a pond and tennis courts. Besides playing tennis, my father mentioned hunting with his father and skiing. He let me look through boxes of the photographs he took on ski trips to the Arlberg Alps in Austria in 1928 and to Norway in 1936. Many of the photographs look like they were taken from an airplane window, as all you see are mountain peaks and great, sloping expanses of untouched snow. There are no crowds or ski lift lines. In fact, there are no lifts. My father spoke of hiking up and skiing down—from the look of the Alps, there must have been much more hiking than skiing! There is the occasional photo of a ski lodge and many pictures of his skiing companions—mostly photos of attractive women in woolen skirts, although a few wore pants. They were all lean, muscled athletes—no snow bunnies on those slopes! My father was in his twenties and early thirties at the time. I later learned that his family worried that he might never marry because his friends were mostly Christian, and after 1935, it was illegal for him to marry a non-Jew.

In thinking back, I see that there was a major difference in the autobiographical stories told by my father and by my mother. At bedtime, after reading from the fairy tale and poetry books I loved, my mother was willing to share detailed stories of her childhood. My father did not do this, but he knew how to invent stories and plied me with tales of funny rabbits and goats. I loved his made-up stories and forgot to ask for the real ones. My favorites involved three rabbits. One was named Fft, one was named Fft Fft, and one was Fft Fft Fft.

My father was freer with stories about his early years in this country where he embraced his new life with gusto. He told of watching movies to learn English and of his newly acquired obsessions with ketchup, which he poured liberally on everything, and baseball. In an envelope labeled "New York 1938," I found photos of my father swinging a bat while sporting a button-down white shirt tucked into belted slacks. His teammates are similarly dressed, but with rolled-up sleeves. They appear to be playing on an urban lot, perhaps on a work break. I have the certificate granting him secret clearance for his job with the United States Army during World War II in the Division of Chemical Warfare and a photo of him in his tan army uniform. For most of his career, he worked in private industry for a chemical company where he also met my mother. He was forty-nine and she was twenty-nine, a first and lasting marriage for both until my father's death from colon cancer in 1980 at the age of seventy-eight.

As the child of a first-generation German immigrant, I learned early on that, in some eyes, to have German genes was to be tainted with a lingering evil. When occasional anti-German remarks would be made in my presence, I remembered my father had helped the Allied efforts against Hitler. To my great relief, his German hands seemed clean of Jewish blood. My first-year college roommate, who was Jewish, later told me how upset her father had become when he read the letter with roommate assignments and saw my name. How could the school match his precious daughter with a German?! When our son, named Hans Gregorio for his grandfathers, remarked that he was thinking about getting a tattoo of the German and Argentinian flags to honor his dual ancestry, he was warned that some people might think he was a neo-Nazi. He didn't get the tattoo.

While I was growing up, we hung no flags but definitely celebrated our German heritage, which was on my mother's side as well. Three of her great-grandparents emigrated from Germany in the nineteenth century. I knew my father arrived on these shores with little beside his trunks, his education, and the address of a family friend. In the trunks were some treasures from the home he grew up in—linens and silver, books and some art—nothing more. My mother called it his trousseau.

I had German children's books, song books, dolls, and dirndls. My parents taught me a little German, but to my regret, I did not become fluent. My parents were told that speaking two different languages would confuse me and they accepted this thinking. The only books I could read in German were written for toddlers, like *Wo Ist Bubi?*—"Where Is Bubi?"

Confusing cuisines was never a worry. My parents gave German-themed parties filling our house with the smells of grilling *wurst* and homemade sauerkraut simmering on the stove along with big pots of kale and potatoes. My job was to chop the apples and onions and add the juniper berries to the sauerkraut. At Christmastime, I helped my mother make the cookies my father remembered from his childhood. Family friends always sent us marzipan, for which my father's hometown of Lübeck is famous, and there was *stöllen* for Christmas breakfast along with scrambled eggs and smoked eel, a tradition from northern Germany near the Baltic Sea. Eel was not on most New Jersey Christmas menus, and my mother went on an annual quest to find it. I remember the year I was thirteen, and the search had proven unsuccessful. My mother and I were doing some last minute Christmas shopping at Bloomingdale's in a nearby mall when I spied smoked eel in a refrigerator case where food delicacies were being sold. I couldn't believe my good fortune—eel at Bloomingdales! Without her knowledge, I bought it and hid it in the back of the refrigerator.

A few days later, on Christmas Eve, I presented the package with tremendous pride; my father would be able to enjoy smoked eel on Christmas morning, just like he did in Lübeck when he was my age. I waited excitedly as my very pleased father took his present to our kitchen and opened the many layers of plastic wrapping. As the final piece was peeled off, the eel was revealed, gloriously plump and glistening!—and emanating a sickening odor. The eel was rancid. I was thankful that my mother did not say what she must have been thinking—Bloomingdales is not the best venue for eel shopping.

Although culinary nostalgia was ever-present, the church had an even more prominent place in our lives. It was my father who insisted on joining the Lutheran church. It was my father's confirmation certificate, from 1918, that hung proudly on my parents' bedroom wall, a vestige from the days when church certificates were works of art. In this one, Peter grasps Jesus' billowing robes, pulling himself up from the waves where Jesus stands calmly and speaks, "Do not fear, it is I." The old certificate is marred by a brown water stain that now seems ominous.

On their honeymoon in 1953, my father brought my mother to the magnificent brick gothic church where he was baptized and confirmed, St. Mary's Church in Lübeck, still bearing the scars of an allied bombing raid in 1942. My mother recalled standing in the church and looking up past the columns and arches right into the sky. The roof had not yet been repaired at that time. Several years before I considered seminary, my father gave me a book of sermons by the German pastor and theologian Helmut Thielicke. He raved about Thielicke's ability to connect with university students and professors, farmers and shopkeepers alike. He joined the throngs who gathered to hear him preach and admired the pastor's brave repudiation of Nazi propaganda. It was a high homiletical bar from my father who died two years before I was ordained as a Lutheran pastor, but not before handing over the spiritual inheritance that has shaped my life.

My father imbued parental maxims like "Don't follow the crowd!" and "Stand up for what you believe!" with a fierce urgency. His mantra to "be yourself" come what may makes me wonder if his own identity issues were so deeply buried that they had ceased to exist for him. On the other hand, the very thing he wanted to keep from me was not always far from the surface. When I was in high school, a friend of mine became very involved with the Roman Catholic charismatic renewal, and I began to attend prayer meetings with him. My parents were curious and a bit concerned, wondering if it was a cult, and so they attended a meeting to see for themselves. My father became so upset that he could barely speak, which made no sense to me, even when my mother later explained that it reminded him of a Hitler rally. Something about the group vibe and regulated responses triggered a visceral reaction. At the time, I knew he hated Hitler, but what decent person didn't?

Anyone who knew my father well would say that he could be stubborn to a fault. On some such occasions my mother would refer to him as a "Prussian general." But there was another side to his stubborn streak—he was unshakably faithful to his word, his commitments, and his beliefs. The fact that he could maintain a wall of silence for so many years, even with those he loved and trusted most, is not surprising in one way. If he believed that something was for the best, he would stick with it no matter what. On the other hand, I am not at all sure that it was commitment that led to his silence for all those years. What it was is something that would take time to explore.

***

Sometimes I wondered what my paternal grandparents did during the Third Reich. In 1933, when Hitler assumed power, my grandfather was sixty-seven and my grandmother was sixty-one.

Were my grandparents Nazi collaborators? Were they good people who did nothing? Neither alternative was pleasant to dwell on. I certainly could not imagine my loving grandmother as a Nazi sympathizer, but then, a nation of sweet grandmothers who said and did nothing as their neighbors and their neighbors' children and grandchildren were massacred helped smooth the onward grind of evil.

I assumed that if my grandparents had been among the meager numbers of "Righteous Gentiles"—the German citizens who risked their lives to protest a hateful regime—my father would surely have spoken of it with pride. I took his silence on the subject to mean that there was not much to say. If my grandparents were not active in collaboration or resistance, that left one alternative: that they were caught up in the sweep of horror, riding it out as best they could, sending their own children away to safety and . . . and what? What did they do while the annihilation of millions went on around them? Did they not realize what was happening? It was unbearable to think about.

That there might be another possible position for my grandparents during the Shoah*—that they might have been Jewish victims of Nazi horror—never, not for a fleeting second, entered my mind. But it was exactly there in that inconceivable, unimaginable place that my real grandparents were to be found. In the internet frenzy brought on by my daughter's discovery, I located the manifest for the ship that brought my father here. The S.S. *Europa* docked in New York harbor on June 2, 1938. On board was Dr. Hans Neumark, age 35, engineer, nationality: German, race: *Hebrew*. The last was surely

---

*I have chosen to use the word "Shoah" rather than "Holocaust," which comes from the Greek for "burnt offering." Many have come to find "Shoah," which is Hebrew for "catastrophe," to be more accurate and appropriate.

typed in against his will, taken from his German identity document. He did share a memory of that voyage with me, a photo of the day he set forth. Friends had come to the dock to see him off, and they are all smiling and waving up toward the big ship where my father, already on board, snaps their picture. There is nothing to see except that it is a lovely, sunny day for adventure. My father could never have imagined the day years later when I would sit here with the ship's manifest before me, his secret exposed by Ancestry.com. The trunks of family silver and linens, his photographs and artwork, his German culture and the faith he practiced were all passed down, but not this: my father was Jewish. He was descended from a Jewish family that can be traced back to the seventeenth century, and perhaps further.

I realize that I have clues and resources to trace my father's journey that others do not. I think of eight-year-old Miguelito hiding his tears under a table during our church homework help program. When I took him aside, he told me that he was missing his mother. Miguelito came here from Mexico with his parents and older sister. One day, he arrived home from school and his mother was no longer there. He knows she's back in Mexico, but he doesn't know why and no one will talk about the situation. Miguelito is a child but his longing is ageless. Recently, a woman told me about the father her mother has always refused to speak about, "It makes me feel like half of me is missing even at seventy." I take this journey mindful of so many more.

A Boy That Wept

There is a Hasidic tale from Menahem Mendel of Vorki describing the moment from the book of Exodus when Pharaoh's daughter is shown the baby found inside a rush basket, floating in the Nile River:

> "And she opened it, and *saw* . . . a boy that wept." "What we should expect to be told," said he, "is that she *heard* the child Moses weeping. But the child was weeping inside himself. That is why later on we find the words: 'and (she) said: This is one of the Hebrews' children.' It was the Jewish kind of weeping."

My father was Lutheran, but he lived with the Jewish kind of weeping. He adjusted to his new life on these shores, and when he got news of his parents' deportation, the sacking of their home, and eventually his father's death in Theresienstadt and his mother's liberation, he took all that he felt to some private place and locked it in. Soon after Ana's discovery, I spoke with my parents' closest friends, and they were all stunned. My mother's sister, her only sibling, with whom she shared most everything, had the same reaction.

I could not ask my mother, who had died two years earlier, but I am certain that she did not know. Even if she had promised to carry my father's secret to the grave, I'm sure she would have eventually told me. There is also another reason I believe that she didn't know. My mother was very engaged in genealogical research and, when my father was alive, she told me multiple times of her frustration with his unwillingness to help with his side of the family. She was disappointed and annoyed with his lack of interest in the past. She said that she was going to focus on her ancestors, and when she finished with that, she would try again to get his assistance. She died before completing the research into her own roots and would never have made the comments she did had she known the truth about my father.

It's difficult for me to understand how one could be in a thirty-year, intimate relationship and never speak of something of such a profound impact. I can imagine that when my father first arrived, he may have been anxious about anti-Semitism here. One of his friends told me that it was not uncommon, even through the 1950s, to find job opportunities in the paper listed as "Chr only." By the time my father met and married my mother, he had already been here for more than ten years and was well into building a new life and a new identity for himself. He may have feared my mother's reaction. He may have internalized a sense of shame. He may have viewed his history as a burden that he did not want to impose on his young wife and, later, on me, his daughter. He may have dealt with trauma by burying it beyond speech. In the end, my father's silence may have gone beyond his conscious control. I spoke with a therapist whose own father is a Shoah survivor and whose grandmother was killed at Auschwitz. He mentioned that my father may also have felt guilt for leaving his elderly parents, even though he could have done nothing to save them.

Outwardly my father was highly successful, like his own father. Upon his arrival here in the summer of 1938, he quickly found work thanks to a family friend in the chemical industry, Gustav Luttringhaus. Uncle Gus was born here to parents who emigrated in the late nineteenth century, but he returned to Germany, where he and my father were chemistry students together in Munich in the 1920s. Some of my father's trauma likely began during this time when German universities were known for increasing anti-Jewish rhetoric and agitation among students and professors.

In 1923, when my father and Gus were studying there, Munich was the site of the Beer Hall Putsch, Hitler's first attempt at a government coup. Hitler, accompanied by six hundred storm troopers, crashed a large beer hall where several thousand were gathered for a speech. He announced that the Nazis had taken over the state government, a first step toward national control. This was not true, and armed police and soldiers were able to thwart the effort; nevertheless, it was a chaotic and violent few days. In addition to speeches in the beer hall, Hitler's backers rallied the crowds gathering outside. The main speaker out in the plaza was Julius Streicher, who later became one of Hitler's propaganda publishers. Streicher even spread the message of hate to young children with books like *The Toadstool*, that compared Jews to alluring, but poisonous, mushrooms.

Jewish young people at the university must have felt especially vulnerable and afraid as they saw three to four thousand of their student peers riot and march in protest and lay wreathes outside the beer hall to honor the sixteen fallen Nazis, hailed as martyrs. My father was twenty-one years old at the time, the same age as my son as I write. In this hate-charged atmosphere, he went back to studying chemistry, and how he focused, I do not know. Perhaps he found escape and stability in the world seen through electrochemical windows. Following the failed coup, Hitler was arrested and served nine months in jail, time he used for writing *Mein Kampf*.

My father's friend Gus came back to the United States in 1933. Gus was already working in a chemical lab by the time my father arrived in 1938 and served as his sponsor. My father's path as an immigrant was smoother than many. While still in Germany in 1928, he filed to patent a process for making zinc from oxygen compounds. The United States granted him the patent in 1930. In June of 1938, the same month of his entry, he was hired as a chemical engineer at the Pyrites Company in Delaware. Pyrite is an iron sulfide, and the knowledge he acquired at his father's iron works plant would have made this a perfect fit and place to launch his career here. Within four months, he was hired by the Allied Chemical and Dye Corporation as a research supervisor and later as a technical director. He worked there until his retirement.

During his time at Allied Chemical, my father also served the U.S. government. From April through November in 1945, he worked for the Army's Division of Chemical Warfare. In the 1950s, the Army gave him a "top secret" clearance, and he worked for the Atomic Energy Commission. Later, he was under contract with the Air Force to develop an over-the-highway trailer for transporting liquid fluorine. He also served as a consultant on several projects with NASA.

I had the sense that my father enjoyed his work and found satisfaction in it. He published articles in journals and was recognized in his field. After retiring, he worked as a consultant with the U.S. Department of Transportation almost until his death. My father's final project was to prepare a booklet of safety procedures corresponding to coded numbers placed on trucks carrying hazardous materials. This was so that fire fighters and other first responders would know how to proceed in the event of an accident. To this day, when I see trucks bearing these numbers, I think of my father in his study, bent over the typewriter. While cancer cells went about their secret work, my father labored on, hoping to save lives. The completed, published manual arrived in the mail from Washington shortly after his death.

From almost all appearances, my father was a fulfilled and happy man. He had meaningful work, a good marriage, and a close circle of friends. I could not have imagined a better father, although I sometimes chafed under his inflexibility. My mother understood when white lipstick was all the rage. My father did not. On the other hand, he always encouraged my deepest interests, even when they differed from his own. He bought me countless books of poetry and cheered on my every poetic effort, even though writing poetry was not a practical profession.

When I took a year off from college to work as a church volunteer on Johns Island near the coast of South Carolina, my father drove down with my mother and helped me get settled in the converted garden shed that was to be my home. While my mother and I cleaned the bathroom, my father scraped old fish scales from the kitchen sink, where they seemed to have been cemented like barnacles. The more we cleaned, the worse the place smelled. Finally, my father, the chemist, pointed out that the water must be high in sulphur, giving off the odor of rotten eggs. I boiled it for drinking but that didn't help with showers.

On the island, as in college, I received his regular letters and postcards, filled with parental worry and love. Once, when my parents visited, they went with me to worship at the local AME Zion church. It was August, and even the funeral-home fans were wilting. My father, who hated heat and humidity, looked unbelievingly at his watch when an hour passed and the sermon hadn't even started. Church services were supposed to last a brisk fifty minutes; nevertheless, he stayed and sweated for my sake. I treasured our close bond which makes the knowledge of all that he held back especially perplexing and painful.

There are many children, and adults for that matter, who sense the ghostly presence of unspoken stories in their homes and do not know how to address this. If they ask, they are likely to be shushed. In my case, although I had no clue of the source, I sensed the sorrow in my father's dark eyes. Paul Célan, a Jewish poet who survived the Shoah, wrote afterward that "A strange lostness/Was palpably present." In the years following my father's death, I'd almost forgotten that palpable presence and I'd completely forgotten the poem I wrote when I was seventeen as a gift for his seventieth birthday. When I began my intensive, mental search for past signs of my father's secret, I remembered the poem and found it. At first I was appalled. In it, I compared the villa he grew up in to "an affluent concentration camp/where childhood was not tolerated." It was a particularly ironic and terrible case of the hyperbolic exaggeration to which adolescent poets are prone. Recalling his limited stories of growing up along with some stilted ideas of German culture and upper class family life, I drew on the worst image I could think of. How could I have even thought to write something that would compare the home where my father was loved and raised, where he had every material comfort, beautiful gardens, friends and family, the grand home that was intended to be his inheritance when he took over his father's business—how could I have compared this to a concentration camp? From my privileged, protected childhood, so distant from the real horrors of history, so ignorant of my own history, it was not hard at all. I threw metaphors around irresponsibly, never worrying where they might strike. Even so, I place less blame on my teenage self than on the many adults who make such misbegotten comparisons to the Shoah and should know better.

The poem is also surprisingly prescient. It begins:

Until now
I have been unable
to touch the silence
the shy hideous growth

between you and me
But I could feel its awful passion
and was afraid
Now it is split wide open and
waiting for me like a confessional
I can no longer deny.

I wrote of being "blessed/by the words you can never speak" and of his tears—

Oh your tears your tears
cantabile moons singing pathetically
to the stranger who will inherit
your eyes
the deepest earths.

I cringe at the overblown lines, yet it gives me chills to see how I was awkwardly trying to give voice to the pain I sensed so acutely but could never truly name or understand. My father's eyes were dark pools of unconscious communication that spoke to me, his only child.

What must my father have felt and thought upon reading my poem? It was one of the few occasions when he wept openly. I was pleased. My poetry, which was usually met by my parent's uncomprehending but loving nods, had moved my father to tears. That was thirty years ago, and how I wish it had been different. How I wish his tears had turned to speech. How I long to take this journey back in time with my father beside me, but he has left me to do it without him. When I was a child, people would always say that I had my father's eyes. I will have to use them to look upon those things he did not want me to see.

CHAPTER TWO

WITTMUND

Edzard's Big Hobby

It was May of 2009 when Ana woke me to read the life-changing Wikipedia page, and I could scarcely think of anything else in the weeks that followed. I quickly called Carsten, a friend in Germany who spent time as an intern at my church in the South Bronx, to share the news. I also sent him a link to the Wikipedia article with its footnote indicating that the information came from a book chapter titled: "The History of Jews in Wittmund and the Jewish Family Neumark." The chapter was written by Edzard Eichenbaum and Helmut Hinrich. Soon Carsten called excitedly to tell me that he had looked up the first author through the phone book and had spoken with him. According to Carsten, this author was approaching eighty years old and inexplicably had boxes of genealogical data about my family.

Herr Eichenbaum and I were soon on a first-name basis through our frequent emails, aided by German-speaking members of my congregation. I realized that if I wanted to find out more about my family history, a visit to Wittmund was essential, and perhaps urgent, given Edzard's age. We had been saving for a family vacation to Argentina that summer to spend time with my husband's mother and the rest of his family, who all live there. Instead we decided that Gregorio and Ana would go to Argentina while Hans, who was eager to learn more of his German namesake, would travel with me. It was now August, just three months after Ana's call, and a footnote was sending us across the ocean.

Hans and I flew to Hamburg and got on a train to Wittmund, a small town I'd never heard of until three months earlier, to meet a stranger who evidently knew much more about my family background than I did. Edzard promised that he would be waiting at the station with an orange umbrella, but when we arrived, no one was there. My stomach churned with worry, realizing that Edzard had never given me his phone number. What if he didn't come? We had traveled all this way just to see an elderly man. What if he was sick? Then, a car drove up and Hans spotted an orange umbrella through the back window. Edzard had been delayed by roadwork detours and was extremely apologetic, although he was only a few minutes late. For a man about to turn eighty, Edzard looked remarkably young with thick, white hair combed back and few wrinkles other than the smile lines round his clear blue eyes.

He drove us through farmland, redolent of cut grass and cows, to his home and introduced Gerde, his wife of fifty-one years. They shared a small, sun-filled apartment with an eat-in kitchen, a living room and dining area, a bedroom, and the tiny room that drew us there. This was the hive of Edzard's genealogical activities, with just enough space for a desk, computer, copy machine, books, and a wall of shelves crammed with boxes of files organized by family, all Jewish, including the family Neumark. The topmost shelves held Edzard's earlier collections: dozens of egg cups and snuff boxes, but he no longer had time to devote to such hobbies.

Many of the relevant materials were spread out on the living room coffee and dining tables so Gerde ushered us into the kitchen to eat the meal she'd prepared for our arrival—red cabbage, potatoes, and veal stew. Conversation was difficult as our hosts spoke no English, and I spoke very little German, but that was what we had to get by on. I learned that Gerde had little interest in her husband's genealogical passion but was glad that it kept him busy. She'd spent her entire life in Wittmund, which at its largest boasted a population of five thousand people. Gerde noticed that nineteen-year-old Hans was eating a lot of her potatoes, and she asked me if we had potatoes in New York.

It became clear that we were not going to accomplish much until Carsten arrived. He was generously taking some of his vacation to come and serve as our translator, and he arrived in time for a late dinner. Finally, I would be able to learn why this man who was not Jewish and had no personal connection to my family had done all this research. Over schnitzel, more potatoes and local Jever beer, the story unfolded. Like his wife, Mr. Eichenbaum had lived in Wittmund his entire life, born there in 1931. His friend Henry was head of the local historic association. In the early 1980s, a professor of art history in Kiel wrote to ask if the association was aware of any Jews having ever lived in Wittmund. Henry, who was overly busy, asked Edzard, who had recently retired and had time on his hands, if he would look into the matter. Edzard told us that he'd never had much interest in history, but he was game to try it. He remembered a synagogue directly across the street from his home as a child and recalled that his father had known some Jewish people, although he, Edzard, never did. He said that he had no idea of how to begin but decided to start by looking up real estate records, street by street.

Since 1819, fire insurance records were kept for every home with information about who lived there, and the records were in Aurich, a nearby town. "One thing kept leading to another," he said, and so began what Edzard referred to as his big ("*grosses*") hobby.

"Some people spend money building train sets in their basements, and I spend my money on making photocopies," Edzard told us. His operation had not been digitalized at that time although he had begun to use a computer for email and a bit of scanning. Most of his work was accomplished by combing through local archives in libraries and town halls, scouring hundreds of yellowed newspapers, writing letters and waiting for replies. Much of the material he unearthed is not available digitally anyway. I certainly would never have been able to access all that Edzard amassed over his years of meticulous labor. What are the chances that a man with such a peculiar passion would surface in this little town of my ancestors?

* * *

The next day, Edzard took us to two cemeteries. The first included a memorial built for the Jews from Wittmund known to be murdered under the Third Reich. Before opening the gate to enter, Edzard put on a baseball cap and handed one to Hans. I was touched that, with no one else in the vicinity and no Jews living in Wittmund since 1938, Edzard insisted on this gesture of respect. I felt ashamed that it had not occurred to me to tell Hans to bring his Yankee cap which was back at the motel. We followed Edzard down a grassy path lined with trees and gravestones until we came to the memorial. There, under a grove of trees was a wall of forty-eight blocks, each with a name, birth date and place of death: Auschwitz, Minsk, Riga,

Lodz, Brandenberg, Theresienstadt. In the center was another large black wall engraved with a star of David and a verse from the Biblical book of Lamentations (1:12): "Is this nothing to all you who pass by? Look around: Is there any suffering like the suffering inflicted on me?"

As we approached the memorial and Hans found his great grandfather's name, I realized that I had neglected to bring any stones. It was powerful to see the stones already left behind and to know that in this secluded village, others had made a pilgrimage to honor one of the forty-eight as we were doing. I like the Jewish practice of leaving a stone to mark one's visit to a grave. A stone has greater permanence than flowers. I like the practice, but not thinking as a Jew, it didn't occur to me to bring a couple of stones along, and here there were none to be found.

While I stood with my regret, Hans, who knew nothing of the tradition of stones, was busily scouting the grounds. He returned to anchor something between the bricks by his great grandfather's nameplate. It was a feather, so different from a stone but meaningful in its own way. I silently prayed Psalm 91, one of the few psalms I know by heart: "For he will deliver you from the snare of the fowler and from the deadly pestilence; he will cover you with his pinions and under his wings you will find refuge" (NRSV). The psalm sprang to my mind because of the feather, but as I prayed, I thought—it wasn't true. There was no deliverance from the snare of the fowler, no refuge from the deadly pestilence.

Hans' feather also reminded me of something I'd recently read about *Kristallnacht*, ("Night of Broken Glass"), the Nazi rampage that burned synagogues and destroyed thousands of Jewish businesses and homes on November 9-10, 1938. Ninety-one Jews were murdered and thousands were rounded up for concentration camps, including all the Jews left in Wittmund at the time. What was new for me was reading selections from the memoirs of Jewish women who survived that night. The women shift their descriptive focus from broken glass to flying feathers: "the mobs tore up feather blankets and pillows, shaking them into the rooms, out the windows, and down the stairway." While others seized on the defining image of shattering glass storefronts for public destruction, these women wanted to remind the world of the parallel devastation in their private spaces—ordered homes ravaged as the deadly pestilence tore into every last pillow of comfort and the pinions of solace drifted down into the darkness, no refuge in sight. The words of the psalm fell like dry, useless twigs to the bottom of my heart. We stood silently before my grandfather's stone, now gently touched by Hans' feather: Dr. Moritz Neumark, 2.6.1866, Theresienstadt.

As we walked back, I noticed old gravestones we'd scarcely glanced at on our way to the memorial. The pestilence had attacked them too. Many of the stones were vandalized with the names of their dead hacked off. It was like a second killing, not only taking a person's life, but perpetrating the illusion that they never lived in the first place. We were about to find an even worse form of vandalism at our next stop.

As soon as we parked, Hans and I looked around and pocketed a few stones. Edzard had brought us to the oldest Jewish cemetery in Wittmund. A plaque at the site states that the first official record of Jews in Wittmund dates from 1739. Edzard has been trying to change the plaque because he has evidence of Jews who received letters of protection allowing them to live in Wittmund much earlier. Towns existed to protect their citizens, and Jews were not entitled to such protection unless they received a letter of approval from a local prince and paid a fee for the privilege, in addition to an ongoing Jew tax. Edzard gave me a copy of a letter from Earl Ulrich, dated June 23, 1645. In this document, the Earl gives permission to three Jewish families to settle in Wittmund—the families of Davyt Abrahams, Moyses Nathans, and Gotschalk Isaacs. He then showed us Moyses Nathans on our family tree.

Hans and I were interested to know if we had ancestors buried in this cemetery and were surprised to see that there were only a handful of stones under a cluster of trees. Edzard told us the cemetery in Wittmund had once been crowded with hundreds of gravestones. Where did they go? The Nazis came with a bulldozer and a backhoe. Plundering the holy garden, they dug up the earth to build a bunker, trucking away the sanctified stones like garbage. Only seven stones were ever found and no skeletal remains.

My heart contracted like a fist and sank. It was also disappointing that there was little likelihood of finding our ancestors buried here. Edzard walked toward the seven tombstones and beckoned for us to follow and read the names: Samson Aron Neumark and Josef Moses Neumark. Two of the seven rescued stones belonged to us! Both stones were engraved with Hebrew on one side and German on the other. Of Josef Moses Neumark, who died in 1822, it says:

Here is buried a wise and reasonable man.
His deeds were done out of faith.
He stood fast for justice until his end.
He put his trust in his Lord.
This is our rabbi, our teacher, our mohel (circumciser).
Josef, son of Moses.
He brought in many friends
to the community of God's Israel

A rabbi? Many times people have asked me if I have pastors in my background. To them, it seemed natural that I might, given my German Lutheran heritage. I used to wish for these phantom pastors to emerge from their hiding place and present themselves. I longed to find family in the procession of clergy who went before me feeling that it would lend something to my own call, exactly what, I can't say. Perhaps an opening for those who wonder why anyone today would possibly chose such a career—"Oh, that's where she gets it!" Of course, it's not really a choice, but that's even harder to explain. It wouldn't have occurred to me that I should have been searching for rabbis instead. Josef Moses Neumark was no longer buried there, but his community's testimony remains: "He stood fast for justice . . . he brought in many friends to the community of God's Israel." I felt that he was bringing me closer to my own spiritual roots, my own pastoral call somehow entwined with his. Later, I would find more rabbis on the family tree, including Rabbi Jacob Emden and Rabbi Meschullum Zalman Mirels Neumark from the late seventeenth and early eighteenth centuries. Emden was a well-known scholar who published over fifty works, including a frank memoir which shocked many of his peers at a time when memoirs were a rarity. He was also remarkable for his attitude of respect towards "honest" Christians, believing that Christianity has a valuable role in God's plan for humanity. In the future, when I am asked about clergy in my family background, I will have an answer as improbable as it is marvelous.

Hans and I put our small stones atop the grave-markers of our forebears. For me, the cemeteries matter, not just for genealogical clues, but as testimony, as witnesses after the blood and bones have disappeared. The stones we left were the only ones there, since any placed earlier had been swept away when the cemetery was destroyed. I thought of the prophet Ezekiel who envisioned a field of dry, scattered bones, beyond help:

> "Come from the four winds, breath!
> Breathe into these dead bodies and let them live."
> I prophesied just as (God) commanded me.
> When the breath entered them, they came to life
> and stood on their feet, an extraordinarily large company.
>
> (Ezekiel 37:9-10)

They stand, beyond our field of vision, watching to see what we will do, whether we too will stand fast for justice until the end.

RE-MEMBERING

Edzard's paperwork had carried us back as far as 1645 when the first known Jews and Neumark ancestors settled in Wittmund, but Edzard's research leads him to believe that others arrived earlier, as refugees from Brandenburg in 1510. The original Neumark was a geographical area of Brandenburg, now part of Poland. Jews had been officially permitted to live in the Neumark since the fourteenth century. This acceptance proved fragile and ended abruptly during the Black Death, when Jews became the scapegoats blamed for poisoning wells and performing spells to cause the plague. Persecution and executions followed.

The surviving Neumark/Brandenburg Jews were expelled from the region and then permitted to return if they could pay exorbitant taxes. In 1510 they were booted out again, this time charged with desecrating the host. Since the advent of the Roman Catholic doctrine of transubstantiation (the Communion wafer becoming the actual body of Jesus), Jews had been accused of attacking consecrated wafers, stabbing and piercing them with knives or nails in an attempt to recreate the crucifixion of Jesus. Blood from supposedly bleeding wafers was said to have been used as rouge on Jewish cheeks. Along with these vile fabrications, fantasies were spun about victimized hosts wailing in pain like injured children.

The real victims of this hateful hysteria were condemned and burned at the stake. In Brandenberg, there was a mass trial of those charged with desecrating the host, and thirty-eight Jews were burnt alive. Two others "accepted" Christianity and were rewarded by being beheaded "mercifully." The other four or five hundred Jews were expelled. According to Edzard, and confirmed by other researchers, it was a group of these refugees who arrived in Wittmund in 1510, among them the Neumarks, who settled and lived there for generations to come. If Edzard is correct, my grandfather was a direct descendent of the Neumark Jewish refugees.

How is it possible that I, a descendant of these Jewish outcasts, stand at the altar every Sunday saying prayers of blessing over bread and wine and repeating the words, "The body of Christ, given for you. The blood of Christ, shed for you," as I place the host in the hands of my congregants? I've done it for thirty years without thinking of these slaughtered Jews, my namesake Jews, who died over a perversion of this very sacrament. Now, I cannot do it without their painful presence beside me.

"On the night in which he was betrayed, he took bread." I feel partly like a traitor myself—that I have betrayed my own Jewish kin, albeit unknowingly. And yet I cannot turn away from the altar where for me, in spite of everything I now know, these remain life-giving words. In the face of betrayal and hatred, another victimized, brutalized Jew took bread–bread, not revenge, bread—not a never-ending cycle of violence, *bread.* That is the sustaining hope that emerges from the desecrating slaughter of God's children wherever and whenever it occurs, the hope that life can go on, that one day, we can sit together and share a healing, liberating meal, that shalom is possible.

Communion is a mystery, but it is no more otherworldly than the loaves of bread a congregant bakes in her oven in a fifth-floor walk-up in East Harlem while her toddler bangs pots on the kitchen floor. Or the crisp, handmade tortillas lifted from their basket. Or the golden, fragrant circle of Eritrean bread baked by another church member. Or the tasteless, cardboard-like hosts that are only good because they never go bad and can be used in a pinch if nothing fresher is available—sacramental convenience food. We take *this* bread, we speak the words of Jesus at his last meal, and we eat. We remember and we are re-membered.

Several years ago, I had the opportunity to visit Ethiopia with urban church leaders from around the world in order to learn from one another. A participating pastor from Hamburg, Germany, invited me to join her on a free day. She had arranged for a car and driver to guide us around some of the country beyond the city of Addis Ababa where we were meeting.

On the way back, our stomachs reminded us that we had not eaten all day, and there was no sign of any place to buy food. We didn't say anything because who were we to whine about hunger in Ethiopia? After about two hours, we saw a family picnicking on the side of the road. The driver slowed down and asked us if we were hungry. "Does he know these people?" I wondered. No, he didn't. Confused at our driver's insistence, we got out of the car and followed him. The family looked up smiling, exchanged a few words with our guide and began ripping off large pieces of spongy *ingera* bread, filling it with spicy goat stew and motioning for us to take and eat. Was this hospitality something reserved for foreigners? Our guide told us later that it was his custom to scout for picnickers any time he was out driving and became hungry. I tried to imagine a Manhattan cab driver dropping in on someone else's family picnic. It just doesn't happen—not only because New York City cabbies have ubiquitous opportunities to purchase snacks and meals along their route but also because our boundaries between public and private forbid such exchanges.

Communion has often been perceived as a private act, behind closed church doors, where only the initiated are admitted. This is dangerous because it feeds the illusion that public life belongs to a separate sphere. Luther used an expression, often translated as "two kingdoms," to describe spiritual and earthly realms. After 1933 some Lutheran churches seized upon a self-serving interpretation of "two kingdoms" to support inaction against Hitler. Dietrich Bonhoeffer, a Lutheran pastor who was imprisoned and hanged by the Nazis for participating in an attempt on Hitler's life, was the first German theologian to address this issue in his book *Ethics*. He wrote of "pseudo-Lutheranism" that splits reality into two parts leading to the possibility of "a spiritual existence that takes no part in worldly existence, and a worldly existence that can make good its claim of autonomy over against the sacred sector," as National Socialism was all too eager to do. Bonhoeffer also stressed that the Church does not exist for itself, but for the world: "We are otherworldly—ever since we hit upon the devious trick of being religious, yes even 'Christian' at the expense of the earth," and at the expense of the peoples of the earth.

Luther himself, in writing and preaching about Communion is far from otherworldly. He spoke of becoming "one cake" with God and others, not just other Communion-takers but also "common and one with all other people upon earth." He went on to say, "I give myself for the common good and serve you and you make use of what is mine of which you are in need . . . Therefore when I help and serve you in all need, I am your bread." Luther also spoke against those who would seek a privatized spiritual experience at Communion,

> There are those, indeed, who would gladly share in the profits but not in the costs. That is, they like to hear that in this sacrament there is help, fellowship and support promised and given to them. But they are unwilling in their turn to belong also to this fellowship. They will not help the poor, put up with sinners, care for the sorrowing, suffer with the suffering, intercede for others, defend the truth.

And why is that? Luther reasons, "They are unwilling because they fear the world. They do not want to have to suffer disfavor, harm, shame or death for the sake of the truth and of their neighbors . . . they are self-seeking persons." Luther concludes that only by living in connection to others, not only other Christians but all neighbors, especially those who suffer, are we truly partaking of Communion. We partake in the body of Christ to become the re-membered body of Christ in solidarity with those who are most forgotten. Communion serves the re-membering of all communities, all creation, one giant picnic blanketing the world. For Christians, it is a foretaste of the shalom feast envisioned by the prophet Isaiah:

On this mountain,
   the Lord of heavenly forces will prepare for all peoples
      a rich feast, a feast of choice wines, of select foods rich in
      flavor, of choice wines well refined.

[God] will swallow up on this mountain the veil that is veiling all
  peoples, the shroud enshrouding all nations.
[God] will swallow up death forever.
The Lord God will wipe tears from every face. (Isaiah 25:6-8)

The torture and murder of Jews on charges of desecrating the host is the worst desecration of Holy Communion imaginable. Martin Luther himself contributed to this community dismemberment, negating his own eucharistic theology. What about our fellowship with "all neighbors, especially those who suffer?" The pogrom against the Neumark Jews occurred shortly before the Reformation in Germany, but Martin Luther's hateful writings against Jews were ultimately complicit in the torture and murder of millions.

"On the Jews and Their Lies" should be required reading in Lutheran seminaries, but it isn't. Like many church leaders, I was aware that Luther said some terrible things about Jews, but was ignorant of the details, which matter. It's too easy to lump Luther's writing about Jews with his demonizing of others. The Roman pope ("fart-ass and enemy of God"), bishops ("Pope's vomit") and monks ("lice placed by the devil on God Almighty's fur coat") come in for much more frequent and sustained attack throughout Luther's works, but this is often understood as a valid, if exaggerated, critique of institutional corruption and as a sign of the times and Luther's own scatological predilections, which have been analyzed extensively. His writings about Jews were directed at a more vulnerable population and have ended up serving more diabolical ends. After the Shoah, there is no way to read Luther's comments about setting fire to synagogues and destroying the homes of Jews without recognizing their dreadful reverberations.

My church body delayed far too long but has finally repudiated this vile aspect of our heritage in a formal Declaration to the Jewish Community:

> As Lutherans we feel a special burden in this regard because of . . . the catastrophes, including the Holocaust of the twentieth century, suffered by Jews in places where the Lutheran churches were strongly represented . . . In the spirit of that truth-telling, we who bear (Luther's) name and heritage must with pain acknowledge also Luther's anti-Judaic diatribes and the violent recommendations of his later writings against the Jews. As did many of Luther's own companions in the sixteenth century, we reject this violent invective, and yet more do we express our deep and abiding sorrow over its tragic effects on subsequent generations. . . . Grieving the complicity of our own tradition within this history of hatred, moreover, we express our urgent desire to live out our faith in Jesus Christ with love and respect for the Jewish people. We recognize in anti-Semitism a contradiction and an affront to the Gospel, a violation of our hope and calling, and we pledge this church to oppose the deadly working of such bigotry, both within our own circles and in the society around us.

It's hard to know what else could be said, and yet it doesn't feel like enough. A few years ago, as part of our Lenten repentance, we wrapped barbed wire around the legs of our altar. It was fake and harmless, but quite realistic in appearance. We did the same around our pulpit and baptismal font. It was a scandalous reminder that our holiest things have, at times, been hideously perverted. As I write, the altar where we gather for Communion is covered with a mosquito net. It looks like a gossamer white cloth so you don't immediately realize what it is. No one sleeps under the altar, and even though it's presently mosquito season in Manhattan, we don't need to worry about malaria—except that we do. A net over the altar reminds us that what Martin Luther King called "the network of mutuality" goes beyond the walls of our church, our faith, and our geopolitical borders. We remember and are re-membered, one to another. I now remember and am reconnected in another kind of holy communion to the Neumark Jews who had, for me, been shrouded in oblivion.

A MEETING PLACE FOR THE SAGES

Let your house be a meeting place for the sages, and sit in the very dust at their feet, and thirstily drink in their words.

—Talmud

After visiting the cemeteries, Edzard took us to the site of my grandfather's childhood home, built in 1814. Unfortunately, it was torn down in the 1950s, so we had to look at the photo Edzard had with him and imagine it there, a house set snuggly between other homes and shops in the center of town on Church Street, a substantial building with tall radius top windows on the first floor. Standing there, I felt literally rooted to the spot. People were walking by, but I was held still by the force of my ancestors, my great-grandfather and my grandfather who first drew breath, played, studied, and prayed right here. I feel them with me. I want them to know that I'm taking this journey as much to honor them as to discover myself. The home is gone but the worn cobblestones at my feet remained. I stood in the very dust where they stood and it was hard to move away.

The 1814 house was not just my family's home—it was, for some time, the center of Wittmund's small Jewish community. My great-great-grandfather, Abraham Jacobs, born in 1768, was president of the Jewish community and a key figure in the building of the synagogue. Wittmund's mayor did not want to use taxes for a synagogue, even though the town's Jews had paid taxes for several centuries. Abraham organized a house-by-house collection to help raise funds. The city council still voted to reject the proposal, but Abraham continued to press the matter, and finally the council and mayor gave their assent.

The synagogue was built in 1816. In the two years before it was completed, Abraham and his wife, Sarah, hosted services in their home led by Josef Moses. Although he is called a rabbi on the gravestone we visited, Josef Moses didn't have the education required of a real rabbi, but he served the role, as often happened, in areas where actual rabbis were not available. The Neumark home also provided room for Jewish children to study Torah until 1911 when they finally had their own school space.

My great-grandfather Philipp was born at home in 1819, the last of six children. Like his brothers, he was circumcised by Josef Moses. His parents ran a grocery store. At that time, Jews were limited in the work they were allowed to do, but the family appears to have prospered and the children grew up to work as merchants, shopkeepers and tailors. Philipp and his brother Jacob would eventually register their own business, A. J. Neumark Söhne, operated out of the family home. Edzard found and copied several newspaper advertisements indicating the exact nature of the business. In one advertisement, new fur items had just arrived–Muskrat! and Polecat! In another, there was a special sale on at A. J. Neumark's offering new fabrics, clothing and curtains, special tailoring available, likely through their brother Meyer, who ran a tailoring business out of his home, right next door.

Philipp married Julchen Levy in the late 1850s. A year after the successful business venture took off, in 1866, my grandfather was born, the sixth of their ten children. Moritz was raised in a home that certainly lived up to the Talmud's teaching that a home should be a meeting place of sages. It was a busy hub of domestic, economic, and religious activity. Neumark family members dominated Wittmund's list of synagogue presidents and school teachers. From 1816 until the 1890s, when Philipp, Julchen, and their offspring left Wittmund, fifty-five of the eighty years saw a Neumark as synagogue president. Philipp followed his father's footsteps in that role and also served as a teacher in the school from time to time. To see that I come from such a long tradition of congregational leaders, in addition to the rabbis, makes me wonder if my call is a conspiracy of DNA and a strand of the Holy Spirit—a triple helix. It also makes me question what it would be like for me today as a leader in the synagogue down the block rather than in my church.

There is almost no detailed information about the childhood of my grandfather and his siblings, but eight of the ten survived into adulthood. Almost everything found by Edzard is of public record. There were no diaries discovered, and the voices of women are absent. I only know that my grandfather and his brothers and sisters were raised in a devoutly Jewish home, among a large, close-knit family. Their home was a center of Jewish religious life, and they were taught and surrounded by strong Jewish leaders. This knowledge makes my grandfather's later move away from the Jewish faith feel more tragic to me, if that is indeed what occurred.

In walking back from town to Edzard's apartment, it occurrs to me that it is the first time in over a century that a Neumark is walking through the very streets that once bustled with Jewish Neumarks young and old—and that the Neumark returned to her ancestral village is a Lutheran pastor. Feelings of continuity and discontinuity collide with each step.

In 1866, when my grandfather was born, Jews in Germany had become increasingly integrated into the wider German society. By the time he was five, Germany was unified as a single nation state, and Jews obtained legal equality with increased economic, social, and educational opportunities. In villages such as Wittmund, interactions between Jews and Christians had long been an ordinary part of community life, more so than in the larger towns and cities. In a big city like Berlin, shopping options abounded so that Jews and Christians could go their separate ways. In Wittmund, if you needed a new winter coat (Muskrat! Polecat!), there was only one place to go, and it was owned by Jews. As in any small town, people knew more about one another and relied on each other.

A subtle shift from a predominant Jewish identity toward a German identity can be seen in my family's choice of names. Up until my grandfather's generation, almost all of the names were taken straight out of the Hebrew scriptures: Abraham, Aron, Moses, Josef, Jacob, Samson, Salomon. Oddly, this seems less true of the girls, although Sara was a popular choice. When Philipp and Julchen began to have children, in the mid-1800s, this changed.

I never knew my grandfather to be referred to by any name other than Moritz until the Wikipedia article. Then Edzard showed me a copy of the page in the synagogue's book recording his birth. Someone with beautiful handwriting had dipped a pen in black ink and inscribed the name: "Moses Lazarus." Underneath the name is written, "to be called, Moritz." German Jews were now taking German names. It was true for a number of the siblings: Moses would be called Moritz, Abraham would be called Adolf, Joseph would be called Julius and Sara would be called Selma.

In the Hebrew scriptures, a name change signals a shift in identity. When Abram and Sarai receive God's promise of descendants more numerous than the stars, they receive new names as well, Abraham and Sarah. When Jacob wrestles with an angel and rises from the match as a new man, God grants him a new name. He will no longer be defined by his weakness (Jacob meaning "cheater") but by his strength. Emerging from his struggle with God, Jacob is to be called Israel ("God prevails"). An identity of failure becomes an identity of promise.

The giving of German names to Jewish children also represented a promise—that Jewish children would be fully integrated members of German society, with the same rights and opportunities afforded other German children. Yet for me, it feels that something was lost. A grandfather named Moses Lazarus is quite different from a grandfather named Moritz. The profound religious resonance of Moses Lazarus collapsed in two curt German syllables. The Hebrew melody of his name was swallowed up forever, along with the false promise of acceptance.

* * *

Like growing numbers of Jewish families at the time, Philipp and Julchen had achieved a comfortable middle-class lifestyle and would be able to afford advanced educations for their children. As

far as social harmony went, Edzard handed me yet another photocopy. It was a newspaper announcement dated March 31, 1895.
On that date, Wittmund's Unity Men's Choir sang for the eightieth
birthday of Meyer Neumark, Moritz's uncle. Men's singing clubs
were popular, and in Wittmund, Jews were evidently welcomed in
this predominantly Christian group. The fact that this choir would
honor Meyer on his eightieth birthday is testament to a high level of
acceptance. Meyer, who was a master tailor, may well have been the
tailor of choice for his choral peers.

Philipp sang in the Unity choir, too. Edzard took us into his hive
and dug out a small package. Inside the carefully folded plastic bag
lay Philipp's songbook, meant to be a present for me. Evidently, my
great-grandfather was a tenor because the book is for the tenor voice.
How had Edzard obtained this family heirloom? He said that it was
gathering dust in the town library, and he asked if he could have it.
On the title page, in elegant script, Philipp had written his name.
Some of the songs were secular, but many were not. Philipp was
president of the synagogue, but he sang *Ave Maria* with the choir. It
should be noted that the reverse was not true: the Christian men of
the choir did not sing Jewish songs. Harmony only went so far.

✶✶✶

As Philipp and Julchen's children grew up, they began to leave
small village life behind and venture into the wider world. One by
one, they departed to make their mark and raise their own children.
It was the threshold of a new century, and the future opened before
them with few obstacles in sight. Jacob moved to Hannover, married and would soon provide three grandchildren. Adolf moved to

Dresden and led a manufacturing company. Julius opened a business in Annaberg, a suburb of Dresden. Max directed a gas company in Vienna. Bernhard and his wife Johanna left Germany for Liverpool, where Bernhard set up a business importing and selling pianos. Unfortunately, as happens all too often, the two surviving sisters moved on without record. All I have been able to discover is that Jetta married Jacques Daniels and moved to Aachen.

In 1890, on his seventy-first birthday, Philipp made a lavish gift to the synagogue that included new brass chandeliers, altar cloths, and an elaborate chair for the rabbi. These tangible items would manifest his spiritual legacy among Wittmund's Jewish community. And then, two years later, Philipp and Julchen decided to move to Hannover to be with Jacob. Moving entailed parting with many household objects. On April 7, 1892, according to a newspaper clipping, Philipp and Julchen offered the following for sale: "one almost new desk, one very large table with extensions, one very new English grandfather clock, a wall clock, a glass cabinet, a mahogany cabinet, a chest of drawers, a table with chairs, a wash stand, a wardrobe, silver, curtains, bedclothes, a bread cutter, a flour drum with lid, two big ladders, a set of windows, a garden bench, garden chairs, a trellis for beans and peas, wood to burn, fertilizer, barrels, boxes," and at the end of the list, a boldfaced, not-to-be-missed item: "**one pile of dung.**" In an area that to this day is surrounded by farms and farm odors, I suppose you could never get enough of it. It is also a pungent symbol of Jews leaving rural areas behind for urban centers as parents sought the best education and professional options for their children.

As his parents were moving, my grandfather, who had studied metallurgy at the Technical University of Berlin and the University of Dresden, as well as chemistry in Jena, was completing his education. In 1891, at the age of twenty-five, he received his doctorate from the University of Erlangen. He worked in the production of steel for a few years in Upper Silesia, in an area that is now Poland. Before long, he was asked to leave to build a similar plant in Gleiwitz, now Gliwice, Poland. The town of Zabrze was nearby, a local source of coal for iron production, and it seems, something more. In 1895, the same year of the move to Gleiwitz, an announcement appears, photocopied by Edzard. It shows Moritz's engagement to Miss Ida Händler, daughter of a Jewish brewery owner in Zabrze. My son was excited to find that he had a bonafide brewmaster in his background.

Why is it so compelling to find connections between previous generations and ourselves? I think it may be because it makes our own lives feel less random, part of a larger design and pattern. This is also a boon of what many Christians call the communion of saints. Even if a person cannot relate to past family members for any number of reasons, we belong to another vast community of those who have gone before us. Their witness is so rich and varied that anyone can find sweet points of resonance with some from other times and places who mystically surround us. Those who wish they had a brewmaster in their family have many options including Saint Brigid of Ireland known for changing the dirty bath water of the lepers she tended into excellent beer to delight them and quench the thirst of visiting clerics.

JUDENFREI

Before leaving Wittmund, I wanted to know what happened after my family left. It was our last chance to visit with Edzard, and he invited us over for a hearty German breakfast of coffee, crusty rolls, butter, cheese, sausage, and cucumbers from the garden. As we sat in his living room, I pressed him to share more of his own history and relationship with the Jews of Wittmund who so consumed his energy. He told me that by the time he was born in 1931, no Jews went to school with him since by then they had their own school. He repeated the point that in small towns like Wittmund, Jews were more integrated into community life than in larger cities. There was no Jewish area of town and housing was mixed throughout. He said that in the mid 1930s when Jews were not permitted to hold various jobs and Aryan laws prohibited support of Jewish businesses, people in Wittmund mostly ignored the laws because they were simply not practical. As with winter coats, the only butcher was a Jewish butcher, and that's where you got most of your meat (pork was sold at a separate store). Despite this, Edzard reported no Jewish childhood friends. All of his friends came from his school, and there was evidently no after-school mingling of playmates.

Following Hitler's rise to power in 1933, the already diminished Jewish community of Wittmund dispersed further, some leaving for the United States, Holland, or England. Edzard told us that Nazi propaganda was a normal part of his schooling but that he didn't remember much about it. This was in the late 1930s and early 40s and Edzard said that he was lucky to be part of what he called the "white generation," those too young to go to war. Some people were very strong Nazis, he said, while others didn't seem interested in anything beyond their little town. His father had some "problems" because when Nazis walked by with the flag, he didn't salute. In the end, he got off with only a stiff warning.

Edzard showed me a local newspaper article from June of 1938:

It's unbelievable that unfortunately it still happens that our people cannot separate themselves from Jews all too often, but one case stands out over all. It took place on Sunday afternoon in our town of Wittmund on Mulhenstrasse where some Jewish residents lived. A married couple that was obviously from out of town, from the countryside, visited the Jewish merchant. When they left, they spoke in a very friendly manner to the man, saying: "Ok then, *bis bald!*" ["see you soon"] and "Heil Hitler!"

The "unbelievable" problem was that Hitler's name was dishonored when it was used to salute a Jew.

That same month, Edzard said that a neighbor bought the synagogue. His arthritic fingers curved in quote signs around the word, "bought." In truth, someone confiscated the deed to the property and had the building torn down. People later commented on how lucky it was that no one could later say that the good people of Wittmund burnt down the synagogue. Edzard lamented that he has no idea where the Torah went, since it was not burned. Some think that it was buried, but no one knows and it has not been found. I find it fascinating that this man puzzles over the missing Torah. It is yet another sign of his rare sensitivity to Jewish loss. It moves me that more than seventy years after *Kristallnacht*, here is an old man, not Jewish, still treasuring this Torah, if only by his ongoing rumination on its fate. I myself have grown in my appreciation of Torah scrolls. We only have Bibles that sit on a shelf, like any other book. If one were to go missing, it would be no big deal.

The more liturgical churches do enact ceremonial rites around the Bible. At the beginning of worship, a book-bearer lifts a larger-than-usual Bible in procession and places it on a stand from where it will be read. When the gospel is going to be proclaimed, we welcome the Word by standing and singing. The Bible may be carried to the center of the assembly, accompanied by torches and read from the midst of the people. We remain standing while the gospel is read because we believe that Christ enters with the Word, but standing for the reading may also be a sign of our Jewish liturgical roots. We, however, do not dance with the Bible, and no one clamors to touch the Bible or to kiss it. Although the church has a rich tradition of illuminated manuscripts, and even jewel-encrusted Bibles, they can be seen in museums, not in the buildings where most living congregations gather for worship with their scripture bound in mass-produced pages.

I once took a church confirmation class to visit a neighboring synagogue, Ansche Chesed. The youth were riveted by the Torah scroll that the rabbi graciously removed from an ark. They had never seen accessorized scriptures. The Torah came dressed in an embroidered velvet cloak with a silver breastplate. The cloak opened to reveal a belt buckled around the scroll, which was rolled around two wooden shafts. The rabbi told us that the breastplate and belt were meant to represent garments once worn by the high priest. She showed us a silver crown that could be placed over the top of the shafts and the *yad*, a long, thin pointer shaped like an arm, ending in a hand with the index finger extended. The *yad* is used to help the Torah reader follow the words without actually touching the scroll. This is both for practical reasons, as the parchment and lettering are easily damaged, and as an act of piety.

When we were done, the rabbi lovingly dressed the Torah again and put it away. "Why don't we do that?" the class wanted to know. I suppose there are many reasons. We don't have precious handwritten, hand-sewn parchments. We gather around Jesus as the Word made flesh. Our weekly worship reverences scripture and the sacrament of Communion shared at a central altar. Our visual focal point is the cross rather than the *Aron Kodesh* or ark.

And yet, I find myself drawn to aspects of the Torah tradition, not the accessories themselves, but the profound exaltation of text. I resonate with the belief of every Hebrew letter, and even the spaces between them, being charged with infinite meaning. We believe that, as Luther put it, "The Word of God, whenever it comes, comes to change and renew the world." But only in Judaism do I see an alphabet of fire, a mysticism of the letters themselves.

The Holocaust Memorial Museum in Washington, D.C., has the post-*Kristallnacht* remains of a Torah ark from a synagogue in Nentershausen, Germany. The Nazis gouged out the golden Hebrew letters across the wooden lintel of the ark that had read: "Know before whom you stand." God's life in the shining letters makes the desecration and destruction of Torah scrolls all the more horrific, a kind of murder unto itself. Edzard honors this and mourns the loss of Wittmund's Torah, as do I. I also wonder what happened to the legacy chandeliers given to the synagogue by my great-grandfather with such pride and love just thirty years before. Were they wrecked or stolen? I prefer to think of them as trashed rather than gracing a Nazi residence like enslaved luminaries.

* * *

After breakfast, Edzard walked with us toward the center of town. It was a warm, sunny day, and all around us, the sidewalk cafes were crowded with vacationers who'd come for the East Frisian beaches and World Heritage mud flats ten miles away. Nobody else appeared to notice the small plaza beside a bank where a bronze six-pointed star was set in the bricks at our feet, bearing the words: *Here stood the synagogue of our Jewish community, 1816–1938.* This memorial was not created until 1996, and although he didn't say so, Edzard was a driving force behind it. It could easily have said "the" Jewish community, rather than "our" Jewish community and I feel certain that Edzard insisted on *unserer*.

When we walked back to his home, Edzard gave me a book he wrote about the history of the synagogue and another with the history of the Jewish school that remains standing. Both books were paid for by the local bank thanks to Edzard's advocacy. The first has a lovely detailed drawing of the synagogue's interior on the cover. Edzard told me that he's never discovered any surviving photographs, but he had memories of looking in the door when he was seven years old and lived across the street. He commissioned a local artist to make a rendering based on those early memories. Now the original drawing hangs in Wittmund's town hall.

There were no other memories to draw upon as no Jews have lived in Wittmund since 1938. By the time of the November pogrom, only a handful of the Jewish families, whose numbers had once exceeded one hundred, were left. After the synagogue was torn down, they met for services in the old Neumark home. A new owner took over both the house and business and welcomed the Jewish community to meet there as they had done so many years before. This time, Edzard believes that the ten men needed for a *minyan* were probably not there, but some form of worship and teaching continued.

What then happened to Wittmund's remaining Jews in 1938? "The Jews were taken away." I found it curious that a person so focused on detail gave such a generalized description of the event. Was it guilt? Sorrow? Did Edzard himself experience some trauma in that night of terror that he feels unworthy to mention? He was only seven years old at the time. At the end of our visit, right before we left, Edzard stopped on his way to the front door and went into his study. He brought out a copy of a letter stamped, "Heimat!" meaning, "Secret!" It was dated November 10, 1938, and contained the report sent back by the SS men who carried out their *Kristallnacht* mission in Wittmund. Evil is masked with the use of neutral phrases. Jewish people are kept in "protective custody." Jewish men are deported by "group transportation." Cash and goods are protected in "secure custody." To avoid damage to nearby buildings, the synagogue is burned "under supervision of the Fire Brigade."

Edzard described things differently. Jews were taken from their homes and beaten while their houses and stores were looted. They were then herded like animals to a building for cattle near the marketplace, beaten some more, and kept overnight. In the morning, the men were taken to Oldenburg and then to a concentration camp. The women and children were let go, though it is unlikely that they got very far. Indeed, a number show up later on the memorial marking their journey's end in Auschwitz or Ravensbrück or Thereisenstadt.

I wondered aloud that the handful of Jews left in Wittmund were deemed important enough to warrant their own pogrom. Indeed, said Edzard, their lives had no import other than to allow the regional Nazi leaders to get in on the action. After the war, a 1949 newspaper article noted the trial and judgment meted out to the perpetrators who came to Wittmund. Ten men were sentenced to serve three months to a year in prison. The average time served was five months. Two had their arrest warrants repealed for "reasons of mercy." Before long, they could all go on with their lives as if nothing had happened.

Life went on in Wittmund, too, almost as though the town's centuries of Jews never existed, never built homes and gardens, never sold fur coats at a good price and sang in the town hall, never buried their dead and circumcised their babies and prayed in the synagogue. On April 16, 1940, Wittmund was formally declared *Judenfrei* (Jew-free), and it has remained so to this day.

Edzard says the real problem is that no one there today knows any Jews. He organizes the schools to bring classes of children to the memorial every year on the November anniversary of the pogrom. He leads tours and tells the history to anyone who will listen. Edzard acknowledges that hardly anyone else in Wittmund cares about this past, but no one complains about his activities. He thinks that others simply wonder why he bothers. Even his best friends find his obsession a bit odd. He does not appear to be trying to redeem any personal failure. He claims no moral high ground for his efforts. "Some one should do it," he says, "and it fell to me."

CHAPTER THREE

LÜBECK

The Iron Works

After our time in Wittmund, Hans and I took a train to Lübeck, a city in northern Germany where my grandfather planted a thriving steel industry in the early 1900s. We dropped off luggage at our hotel and went to visit my Tante Renate who lived a few blocks away. Renate was my father's cousin. I'd met her several times on trips with my parents, but we never discussed much about the past, at least not the history I was now interested in. Renate had planned to ferry us around to various sites, but was recovering from a heart attack, and her physician son convinced her to settle for inviting us to tea. She seemed much younger than her eighty-seven years. Her husband, Dr. Rohrmoser, was far more frail than she, resting on a chaise lounge while Renate poured tea from a silver tea service and her grand-daughter brought out cakes from Neideregger, the famous Lübeck marzipan emporium. Her son, who took over his father's medical practice, sees patients and lives downstairs from his parents.

Renate refused to speak of the past until we'd had two cups of tea and eaten the marzipan torte and cherry chocolate cake filled with whipped cream. She began by recounting a bit about her own history. Her father Heinrich, one of Oma's brothers, was Jewish, but her mother was not. Renate said that this made her what the Nazis called a *Mischling*, the word used for a crossbreed or mongrel. Already in 1935, when Renate was twelve, the Nuremberg Laws had gone into effect, one of which was the Law for the Protection of German Blood and Honor that criminalized intermarriage and sexual relations between Jews and "Aryans." The offspring of such partnerships were labeled as *Mischlinge,* the defective products of race defilement. For a time, sexism joined racism and children with an "Aryan" father and a Jewish mother had more privileges than those with a Jewish father, like Renate. In an effort to protect his daughter, Renate's father divorced her mother, hoping to sever her ties to his Jewish heritage. In spite of being Jewish, Heinrich received a Cross of Honor for his service in World War I. These crosses were not awarded until 1934, and so, like many Jews who served Germany in that war, he believed that his nation would not turn against him.

As things worsened, however, in 1939 Heinrich ended up fleeing to what was then Rhodesia, where he already knew one other refugee. According to the new laws, he had to give the Nazis all of his money to get an exit permit. As soon as he became established in Africa, he planned to send for the family. Renate was sixteen and never saw her father again. A couple of letters arrived that spoke of his increasing depression and inability to adapt to farm work or find a niche for himself in Rhodesia. Before long, they learned of his death, a casualty of hate as much as if he had died at Auschwitz.

Renate and her mother remained living in Hamburg, an hour's train ride from Lübeck. She was an exceptional student and expected to go to college and perhaps further, but being labeled a *Mischling* meant that this was no longer an option. Like Jews, half-Jewish young people were denied entrance to universities and were also excluded from trade schools. Jewish businesses were being closed down, and there were almost no opportunities for a young person like Renate to pursue her education or find a place in the German economy.

If my well-educated father had been born a decade later, this would have been his fate as well: "It was so hard, no one can understand. To be told every day you have no worth, no intelligence, that you are worse than a worm, to be told over and over. No one can understand how hard it was." Renate spoke these words in reference to my father when she was describing him to me as a "burnt child," but I believe she was also speaking of herself. She and my father were both burned by the message of the times.

I am no stranger to "burnt children." The young people in the shelter at my church have all been scorched by hateful labeling and worse. One night at dinner, when Jose was thirteen, he told his mother that he was gay, and she began stabbing him with her fork while yelling, "This is a Christian home!" He has a row of scar bumps on his arm and another on his side from the fork attack. Jose ran away and survived one way or another until he found his way to our shelter. We always celebrate the birthdays of our residents and Jasmine had requested a strawberry cheesecake, but when the day came, she was in the hospital with severe sickle cell anemia. I brought her the cake, but what she really wanted was for me to call her mother. When Jasmine was sixteen, her church-going mother had given her an ultimatum, date boys not girls or pack your things. Before long, Jasmine was forced out on the street. Now she lay hospitalized on her twenty-first birthday, longing for her mother. She asked me to make the call, thinking that her mother might listen to me, a pastor. Instead, I heard her mother say, "I have no daughter!"

The transgender youth have a particularly difficult time finding acceptance even among their gay peers, and it's also harder to find work. In New York, as in many states, such discrimination is legal. Our church and shelter are located on Manhattan's Upper West Side, an area that many would consider a bastion of liberalism, but all of the youth are targets of daily demeaning remarks as they walk the streets and avenues of this neighborhood. Jay told me of going for a walk in a nearby park after a heavy storm. The ground was strewn with broken branches and splintered wood. He became aware that a group of youth was closing in around him and felt trapped as they began calling him names and mocking him: "What is it? Is it a guy or a girl?" Then they began throwing branches and wood chunks at him. Jay keeps a cell phone at the ready for such occasions. He had no more minutes left on it, but pretended to dial 911 and his attackers dispersed. Nineteen-year-old Nicole's attackers did not give up so readily. She required reconstructive facial surgery after a beating that left her permanently brain damaged. The rate of attempted suicide among transgender youth is reported as being upward of fifty percent. A young transgender woman who grew up in a Mormon community in Utah came back to the shelter one night and began to play our piano. When I complemented her on the music, she paused, looked at me, and said, "This is the only place I feel human."

It is galling to know that in almost every case, these young people have been burnt, not helped, by religion. I never imagined that my own privileged family harbored those who'd been taught it was dangerous to claim their full identity. Now I wonder if I, a pastor and the executive director of a shelter for queer youth, have been unknowingly seeking to heal the wounds that also seared my heritage?

* * *

Closeting her identity is how Renate survived. In 1942 she was admitted to a typing school, far from her dreams, but better than nothing. The director told her to never let anyone know she was a *Mischling*. She didn't and was not found out. Soon after her graduation, she met her future husband thanks to a bad bout of hepatitis. During the war, Hans Georg Rohrmoser served as a doctor, caring for the wounded. Renate wanted to be sure I understood her husband had not been in the Nazi party, that he hated National Socialism but had worked strictly as a doctor caring for wounded soldiers. Nevertheless, he was imprisoned for two years in England.

Upon his release, Hans Georg made his way back to Germany and sought work at a hospital in Lübeck, but nothing was available. At that point, he had lost even his ration card and begged for anything. The hospital allowed him to stay on for three weeks—which turned into seventeen years. Renate's brother-in-law, Karli, worked in the same hospital, and so, when Renate became very ill with hepatitis, her sister brought her there. Renate was one of Hans Georg's first patients, and as he tended to her health, they fell in love. Six decades later, she is caring for him. After sharing this personal history, Renate told us how it was that Moritz and his family came to Lübeck.

At the beginning of the twentieth century, Lübeck was experiencing a major growth spurt as the city's importance shifted from trade to industry. I knew that my grandfather had built an iron works plant, but I had no idea how important he was to this pivotal economic shift. Renate explained that her maternal grandfather had connections in Sweden. Moritz and he discussed the feasibility of bringing iron ore from the mountains of Sweden by way of the Baltic Sea. Coal could come from Poland, England, and the Ruhr region of Germany. Moritz was able to secure investments totaling millions of marks. Most, if not all, of the investors were Jewish. Moritz went to the appropriate city officials to present the idea and was given the final go-ahead in 1905.

In early 1906, my grandfather was appointed as the sole director of the iron works that would eventually provide all of Lübeck's electricity and most of the city's industrial jobs. The project required extensive work on water—shaping a canal—as well as on land. It took only fifteen months to finish, a timeline that to me seems inconceivable. A book produced for an exhibition about the iron works in 1985 has a photo showing a large crowd gathered for the laying of the foundation stone. Dr. M. Neumark is flanked by the mayor of Lübeck and the builder from Upper Silesia. Other dignitaries are clustered around them beneath flower garlands draped in loops from the scaffolding. The photo is dated May 8, 1906. There is another picture taken little more than a year later when the blast furnace was first turned on. My father and his sister, Susy, stand next to their mother, surrounded by men in bowler hats and wool caps. It is the earliest photo I've ever seen of my father. He is four years old and adorable in a white sailor suit. His facial features are blurry, but the big Neumark ears that I have inherited stick out unmistakably.

Another thing I didn't know about my grandfather is that in addition to engineering the construction of the iron works, he built an entire village for the thousands of workers needed to run the operation. There was housing for workers and for supervisors. There were flower and vegetable gardens, chicken coops, and a well-stocked store that offered goods at better prices than could be had elsewhere. This was a new concept at the time, and the entire operation was deemed to be so inventive and important for the history of the area, that a museum dedicated to my grandfather's work opened in 1985: *Das Industriemuseum Geschichtswerkstatt Herrenwyk,* which roughly translates as "The Industrial Museum and History Workshop of Herrenwyk."

The museum's website explains that "In the 20th century, the district of Herrenwyk developed from a small fishing and farming village to an industrial suburb of Lübeck with the opening of the blast furnace in 1907 and the shipyard, long the most important industrial employers in the city." In addition to providing jobs, all of Lübeck's electricity came from the gas produced by the coal used to power the furnace.

My father died five years before the museum opened. It was strange to imagine the many people with no connection to my grandparents who visited this museum, absorbing information that Moritz and Ida's own flesh and blood knew nothing about. But now, at last, Hans and I were on our way there.

When we arrived in Herrenwyk, we were greeted by Egbert Staabs, a retired pastor whose work focused on urban ministry and industry. The iron works was still in operation when he came to the area, and he knew congregants who worked there and lived in the village. He interviewed them about their experiences so that the exhibitions and accompanying book could tell the story "from below," from the perspectives of the workers and their families.

Besides detailing the history of living conditions and life in the village, the museum has a section devoted to my grandfather's biography. You can also follow the step-by-step process of producing fine iron ore. Other minerals were found in the ore, including gold and, more commonly, copper. For several years, my father headed the company's ancillary copper production.

I know my father would have been thrilled to see the museum displays, omitting the final one showing the untimely removal of my grandfather and his subsequent internment and death at Theresienstadt. There is also a display of photographs and documents from 1939 to 1945 when prisoners of war and others were forced to labor at the plant under brutal conditions. One testimony from that time begins, "I remember only tears and sorrow."

Throughout our visit to the museum, Hans and I felt like minor celebrities. Photos were snapped of us writing our names in the visitors' book and at other points. I was glad that Pastor Staabs told me he believed that the plant and village combination was a positive model for the sake of workers. He said that many of the workers came from poor areas of eastern Germany and recalled one man telling him that after laboring with virtually no time off, coming to Herrenwyk was a welcome change. He recounted that he had humane hours, his own garden, a pig and geese. He said that he enjoyed free time and holidays and that his children had a good life and were happy.

There was a world of difference between the upper-class lifestyle and privileges enjoyed by my grandparents, my father and his sisters, and the workers at the iron works; nevertheless, I am heartened that Moritz showed concern for his employees' quality of life significantly beyond what was considered necessary or usual at the time. He provided homes and jobs for thousands of people for almost thirty years. This place was primary in his heart and soul and shaped my father's own vocational dreams.

There was a large container for display purposes filled with round iron pellets, an end-product of the operation. I asked if I could take a few, and they said that they would make an exception for me and allow it. I took several iron pellets planning to carry one with me to Theresienstadt and the Ohre River. Such objects have a fascinating power, literally power to fasten us to a piece of our identity.

The nearby villa where my father grew up was built at the same time as the iron works and we were able to visit there too along with Renate. At one time, it had been converted into an apartment building, but the new owners restored it as their private residence. They generously welcomed us for a brief tour. We saw the kitchen where my father ate *Rote Grütze* on laundry day. Renate pointed out the place in the front hall where the children would come in their nightgowns to have a bedtime snack of bread and chocolate with Oma and Opa, who sat in two chairs and told funny stories, as my own father used to tell me. It made me wonder if Fft, Fft Fft, and Fft Fft Fft had been born right there.

* * *

For many years, my grandparents' Jewish background seemed to have no negative impact on their social acceptance. Moritz was elected to Lübeck's senate where he served for over two decades. He had positions on many boards and loved to preside over dinner parties with Lübeck's elite. Around the time they moved to Lübeck, a census showed a population of 633 Jews out of 82,813 people. Of my many questions, one of the most important for me has to do with my grandparents' Judaism. I wanted to know if the surviving relatives of my father's generation knew about it. While in Lübeck, I asked

Renate, and later, in a series of phone calls, I spoke with my elderly cousin Klaus who lives in Brazil. Klaus is the son of my father's sister, Susy, my only living cousin on that side. Renate said that she never noticed anything Jewish at her grandparents' home. Klaus said that his only religious influence growing up was Roman Catholic, because of his father. However, it was not what I would call a practicing Catholicism. His father went to mass once a year on Easter. When they visited his paternal grandmother in Berlin, she insisted that the children accompany her to Sunday mass. He said that the question of Jewishness did not come up for him until 1933, when he was twelve and moved to Berlin with his mother. At home, they prayed regularly before meals, but he said there were never any such prayers at Herrenwyk.

Klaus's only memory of religion with my grandparents was related to the major Christian holidays. On Easter, they hunted for chocolate and marzipan eggs in the garden and ate colored eggs at breakfast. Christmas was the biggest of the celebrations, and each grandchild had his or her own little Christmas tree with presents beneath. The trees had been secretly set up and decorated with candies and real candles. At the appointed time, the locked doors to the Christmas room opened and the excited children, family, and any guests, entered and stood together around the trees and sang Christmas carols before opening the gifts. Klaus said it was a highlight of his childhood. This German holiday tradition is not necessarily indicative of actual conversion. Even Theodor Herzl, the father of modern political Zionism, had a Christmas tree in his home.

For my father, Christmas was both romanticized and profoundly religious. He kept trying to recreate the mythic Christmas of his childhood. In addition to our big tree, I woke on Christmas to find my own little tree with ornaments of candy. My mother searched far and wide to find candies with strings to hang on it. For years, my father tried to get my mother to let us decorate our tree with real candles, dismissing her claim that this was a fire hazard. He said that when he was a child, they would even let him hold a flame to some needles on the tree to fill the room with a nice, piney scent. Those must have been some super-fresh trees! He finally demurred when my mother found realistic-looking electric candles for our tree. We never tried the live-flame tradition.

Christmas was clearly a magical time for children at the villa, though not particularly a religious one. This was never my experience growing up. Although we enjoyed many cultural German Christmas traditions, worship services were always central, as was true for Easter. There was no question but that the special things we enjoyed on the holiday were because it was a holy day, which also brought special religious music, prayers, and worship services.

According to Klaus, this was never true at Herrenwyk. He said that on Christmas and Easter, the family did not attend worship services. In fact, he had no memory of his grandparents ever attending church, saying that "Nobody ever went to church there." Renate said the same thing. What about Judaism? Both Klaus in Brazil and Renate in Germany said there was never a trace of it: no object and not a single thing done or said that they ever noticed. Klaus added that they never had "those things by the door," apparently referring to mezuzahs with Torah portions inside that Jews fasten to their doorposts. He mentioned that he had seen mezuzahs in the homes of family friends but never at our grandparents'. I pressed the point, hoping for something, anything more, but there was nothing. The childhood memories of Klaus and Renate may not be completely accurate, but at this point, I have no other memories to draw on.

What happened to the Jewish boy from Wittmund? The descendant of rabbis and synagogue presidents? Some will say that the trajectory that led to my father's baptism is utterly unremarkable. Many Jews assimilated. Many Jews converted by choice. Many Jews lived as secularized Germans. But to me, it is momentous. It is the reason for the faith that has shaped my life. And also, a break with Judaism in Germany, in the years leading up to the Third Reich and during it, has particular consequences and reverberations. I feel compelled to try to reconstruct the narrative, as best as I can, of what occurred.

THE FONT AND THE PIT

Once a hole opens in how you've been looking at the world, everything else pushes through.

—Ursula Hegi, *Children and Fire*

It's the oldest thing that survived the firestorm that destroyed much of St. Mary's cathedral in Lübeck on Palm Sunday in 1942. In retaliation for the Luftwaffe's bombardment of England's Coventry Cathedral, an Allied bombing raid targeted this jewel among German churches, the world's highest Gothic cathedral built of brick. Much of the church and surrounding buildings burned, but the 1337 bronze baptismal font emerged intact from under the mounds of fallen bricks and ashes. St. Mary's stands tall beside Lübeck's town hall like a protective elder sibling. Like siblings, there has been a strong connection between the two and the spiritual and political powers they represent. St. Mary's was the church of Lübeck's leaders, a proud and, at times, disastrous position.

I visited the church before as a child, but now I came with a new interest in the font where my father was baptized. The first time Hans and I went to St. Mary's, the font was in a roped-off area of the nave, inaccessible to the public because of its age and value. I returned the next day and found a pastor in the church offices next door. He graciously escorted me back to the church and past the rope.

The font is so large that I could easily fit inside it, albeit awkwardly. The basin is held up on the broad shoulders of three kneeling angels who bear its weight with ease. I lay my hand on the baptistry's cool metal, meditating on the connection between my life and the waters that parted for my father's baptism long ago. Where I stood beside this font, my grandparents had come bearing their toddler. For me, it is a place of contradictions: a pool of joy clouded with lament, a well of life-bearing waters bloodied by hatred.

My father was baptized in 1904, when he was two years old. It says so on his confirmation certificate from 1918. In 1908, his sister Lore was baptized as a baby of three months old. Both baptisms occurred around the time that my grandfather was named to build and direct the iron works plant. Although a person can be baptized at any age, it was customary for Lutherans to baptize their offspring as infants, as happened with my Aunt Lore. Since my father's baptism did not occur until the family arrived in Lübeck, it seems likely that the two events were connected.

The move meant greater economic opportunity and social prominence. It meant securing the future for a growing family. This security came with a cost. I believe that what occurred at that font was more an act of assimilation than an act of faith and that it came after a period of gradual distancing and secularization rather than conversion. My grandfather left Wittmund and was educated in universities that began as Christian universities. There was no Hillel House on campus. He was a young man striking off on his own. He left a tightly knit, rural community steeped in the daily, familial rites and customs of their Jewish faith and identity. He entered an increasingly secular environment that probably fed his intellect more than his heart. He was not alone on this path. At the time, many young German Jews were moving from villages to urban areas with enhanced educational, social, and career opportunities.

Despite new possibilities, Jews still faced discrimination, particularly in certain professions. Not a few sought to break through by baptism. This was especially true among Jewish university graduates. The most difficult professions for Jews to enter were university professorships, teaching, and serving as judges. Although my grandfather received his doctorate, I have no evidence that he ever hoped to teach at a university, but in pursuing his career and later in educating his children he likely experienced this same pressure to convert. Moritz received his doctorate in 1891. He wished the same for his son. Between 1880 and 1919 in Germany, there were 16,479 recorded baptisms of Jews into the Protestant church, including the baptisms of my father and his two sisters.

· It's unclear whether Moritz and Ida were ever baptized themselves. Ida's Jewish roots ran as deep as her husband's. Her family's brewery restaurant housed services on major religious holidays and the rooms in her childhood home were used as a *shul* when needed, just as occurred in my grandfather's home. The synagogue was right behind the brewery and across the street was a community prayer room and *mikvah*, the bath for ritual immersion where my grandmother would have immersed herself in preparation for marriage. Did she return to those waters following the birth of my father? I think it likely as the family still lived nearby and my father would not be baptized for two years.

Whether or not my grandparents themselves were baptized, I don't believe that they experienced a religious conversion. True converts tend to be particularly dedicated and passionate in practicing their new faith. Klaus and Renate remember no table prayers and no Sunday church going. On the other hand, their memories are twenty years later than my father's. I know that he went to church with his family, but I don't know how often. Maybe they stopped going when the children were grown. Klaus also said he assumed that our grandparents were baptized because his mother, Susy, was brought up to be Lutheran.

The memories passed down in other branches of the family were different. Uli, the widower of Klaus' sister Ursula, told me before he died that the conversion was "terribly complex." He couldn't elaborate on that. His daughter said that my Aunt Susy considered herself to be a non-practicing Jew and that perhaps the family was still actively Jewish when the children were very young. This wouldn't make sense if my father was baptized at the age of two, unless they had him baptized and continued to practice some degree of Judaism at home for a while. Klaus and Renate had not yet been born at that time. They both expressed great surprise that my father had been confirmed when he was sixteen. Confirmation required several years of study and preparation with the pastor. To them, that indicated a Christian faith commitment of which they were not aware.

Klaus and Renate each said that my father didn't know he was Jewish until the family told him. Neither of them was sure of my father's age when he received this news, but they agreed on a range between late adolescence and early young adulthood. Whatever the precise age, it was a key stage of identity formation, and it corresponded chronologically to the formation of the Nazi party and a post-World War 1 wave of anti-Semitism. In fact, my cousins said that my father was told because the family wanted to be sure that he didn't become enamored of Hitler. My father was not a Jew who rejected his Judaism. Like me, he knew nothing of his Jewish roots, but for him, the revelation must have been far more shocking and disorienting because it was life-threatening news. As my father moved into adulthood, finding his own identity, it was increasingly dangerous to be who he was.

I realize that my reflections on all that led my grandparents to the font are a mix of fact and speculation. It's also true that much of what happened in my family is not unique. Nevertheless, the fact that such Jewish baptisms were increasingly common does not make them any less tragic. These baptisms were only unremarkable because anti-Semitism was business as usual, a force so powerful and twisted that it could lead people raised as Jews, from generations of Jews, to bathe their children in waters stained with the blood of Jews.

As a pastor who has performed hundreds of baptisms, rejoicing in every single one, I find myself in a very unexpected and undesirable place. The deep hollow of St. Mary's bronze font has opened a hole in my heart—and in the heart of my theology. After two years of research, reflection, and writing about my Jewish roots, I heard a lecture given by Dr. Avivah Zornberg, who teaches Torah in Jerusalem and has written a number of books that incorporate Biblical commentary with psychological insights. Her lecture was titled: "An Event Without a Witness: Trauma and Healing in the Joseph Narrative." I later discovered similar material in her book, *The Murmuring Deep: Reflections on the Biblical Unconscious*. Dr. Zornberg's interpretation allowed me to find my own story in Joseph's. In fact, it breaks open the story for anyone who feels that their cry is unheard, their trauma silenced, or their identity masked.

The Joseph narrative is the longest drama in the Hebrew scriptures. In its barest outline, Joseph is favored by his father, Jacob, who has a special robe made for him. This favoritism inspires the jealousy of his older brothers. One day, when they are out in the wilderness tending the family flocks, they see Joseph coming toward them and decide to kill him and dispose of his body in a pit. Instead, one of the brothers, Reuben, suggests that they leave Joseph alive at the bottom of the pit, keeping their hands clean of bloodshed. They follow Reuben's suggestion and then sit down to enjoy lunch. A caravan of traders approaches, and the brothers see another opportunity. They sell Joseph to the traders who take him to Egypt as a slave. Following lunch, the brothers return home and present their father with the remains of Joseph's robe, which they have dipped in goat's blood and ripped apart so that Jacob will think his beloved child has been torn to pieces and devoured by a wild animal.

Joseph survives the pit and many further trials in Egypt where his intelligence and talents lead him to unimaginable success. He becomes the royal administrator over all Egypt. When a severe famine strikes, many people travel to Egypt seeking the food under Joseph's control. His own family is among them, leading to the reunion of Joseph with his brothers and his father. I have heard this story often, preached it and taught it in church. I have watched the children's musical video version multiple times. It never before lay hold of my heart and squeezed the breath from my lungs.

Zornberg zeros in on what is left out. For instance, when Joseph is first thrown into the pit, he does not yell. He does not beg his brothers to release him. He simply disappears into the shadows without a sound. Twenty years later, when the famine drives his brothers to Egypt, they bow before Joseph without any recognition of who he really is. Joseph decides to put them to a test. They must leave one brother behind in prison, take home the grain Joseph gives them, and return to show him their youngest brother. Knowing how their father will react if they show up minus another brother, they said to one another, "We are clearly guilty for what we did to our brother when we saw his life in danger and when he begged us for mercy, but we didn't listen. That's why we're in this danger now" (Genesis 42:21).

Zornberg points out that there never was any begging for mercy. The perpetrators did not allow themselves to hear any crying and so the crying is not recorded: "Joseph and his screams have been absent from the historical moment by the pit. Indeed, to be thrown into a pit in the wilderness is to have one's cries go unheard: one disappears and one's voice is lost." Joseph, Zornberg says, "is like a non-sufferer . . . the narrative of his suffering is erased. . . . His anguish by the pit goes unrecorded precisely because the brothers did not hear it."

This is a familiar story for many families. Early in my ministry, a twelve-year-old girl who attended our Sunday School came into my office to tell me that her uncle was molesting her. She lived with this uncle and her grandmother, and I went to their apartment when the uncle was at work, certain that the grandmother would side with the child. It was a rooky mistake with grave consequences. By the time the police arrived, the family had vanished. Fifteen years later, a young woman came to my office. I didn't recognize her until she told me who she was. She'd run away from home and worked as a dancer in a strip club, dependent on drugs to blunt her pain. Now, she'd been clean and sober for six years, gone to school, gotten a job, and was happy. She said that she'd come to thank me. I was stunned. Whenever I thought of her over the years, I mentally kicked myself and wished I could ask her for forgiveness. What could she possibly be thankful for? "You believed me." She taught me that day not only about courage, resilience, and generosity of spirit, but also that having someone hear your story and believe it makes a difference. Having your cry from the pit ignored or unheard violates a core in our identity and can leave a person distrustful of their own voice and perception of reality.

Like many before and after, Joseph's brothers did not listen. In pondering Zornberg's attention to the missing voices in the text, I think of my father's silent tears. I think of the suffering and terror erased from the narrative of my family history, the absence of any testimony. My grandparents were left in the pit as non-sufferers. They disappeared for decades. Like Joseph, my father was not physically torn to pieces, but another kind of dismemberment did occur. He was cut off from his family lineage. He was taken from his homeland and culture. His internal identity was ruptured. My father's successful scientific career was not exactly the same as becoming the viceroy of Egypt under a Pharaoh, but he did quite well in mid-twentieth-century New Jersey, where a refugee could disappear into the grassy suburbs and emerge on the cover of *Missles & Space* magazine. No one in either place knew or cared about the trauma left behind, the pit without water. The survivors themselves sought to forget it.

Zornberg notes that Joseph named his child Menasseh, which means "forgetfulness": "God has helped me forget all of my troubles and everyone in my father's household" (Genesis 41:51). Yet, when you name your child Forgetfulness, don't you remember every time you call him? My father had the photo of the old villa and many old etchings of Lübeck on the bedroom wall of his new home, an emblem of the past seared onto the supposed blank slate of the present, but how could our home's wallpaper of forgetfulness not provoke memory? Zornberg pins the survivors' disassociation with their own identity on the cruelty of others, citing perhaps the most famous Jewish commentator on the Bible: "As Rashi points out, the brothers had not 'recognized' him at the pit, had had no compassion for him. The result is that he cannot know himself, cannot relate to his past in compassion for himself." I would add that when a person experiences this kind of disassociation due to unacknowledged trauma, it can be extremely difficult to extend compassion to another sufferer in similar circumstances. The grandmother who refused to hear the cries of her own granddaughter may have been abused herself.

Healing, said Zornberg, can only happen when another person hears the truth of what has occurred. Eventually, Joseph's brother Judah comes near to him. Slowly, the words and the tears begin to flow. The Hasidic commentator R. Zodok HaCohen says: "When Joseph revealed himself to them, he no longer hid the light of his face from them. At that moment, they truly recognized him, and were dumbfounded by the light in his face." His father, Jacob, will have a similar epiphany: "I can die now after seeing your face." (Genesis 46:30) Joseph is now seen clearly for who he is. For Zornberg this is the transfiguring moment when a survivor is able to bear witness to his or her own truth. What hope does this hold for my father who was never able to tell his story, who was not able to reveal his true face even to the woman he slept with and adored for thirty years? Nor to me.

I cling to a more muted moment of revelation. "Deep calls to deep," says the psalmist and something from the depths of my father called out to me.

* * *

"Do you renounce the devil and all the forces that defy God?" Every baptism begins with a renunciation of evil. Part of rejecting evil requires us to recognize it, to refuse the comfort of turning away. Now when I stand at our church's font, I see the blessed water, and I see a dry pit with scorpions scuttling around the edges. In baptism we speak of dying to the old self and rising as a new creation. My grandparents drowned their Judaism so their children might rise as newly created Germans, pure as any Aryan. Baptism can even be seen as an assent to Nazi propaganda; being a Jew is no good. How does that evil not scorch the font, leaving it empty and dry like the pit into which Joseph was thrown? What can we say when the water is a mirage and baptism itself becomes a demonic act that defies God?

I'm getting stuck here, and I wish the Church would pause to get stuck with me. I wish we would not just theologize over our inconsistencies. Some will want to remind me that the Church does pause, during Lent. On Ash Wednesday we remember that we are dust and enter into a season of repentance. But I will confess here that I have never considered baptism, the great bath to wash away sin, as a sin in and of itself. I have never considered the remembrance of baptism to be an act of repentance for baptism. In the baptismal rite when we mark the sign of the cross in scented oil on the forehead of the newly baptized, we mark our identity with one who has not turned away from any evil or suffering. And yet, now I have to conclude that in some cases, imposing that mark has been an act of evil.

My father's baptism was a moment of alienation and unrecorded dismemberment. And my father's baptism was an act of saving grace. The font was a place of death and a place of salvation. Out of the pit, Joseph survived. Out of the font, my father survived as well. He became an active member of the body of Christ. He loved the Church and raised me to share that love. Is that not a good thing? Yes and no.

A member of the audience at Zornberg's lecture asked about the part where Joseph says to his brothers in Egypt, "You planned something bad for me, but God produced something good from it, in order to save the lives of many people" (Genesis 50:20). Zornberg interpreted this as a sign of Joseph's own denial of his experience, moving too eagerly to a Hallmark-card ending. I have preached several sermons on this all's-well-that-ends-well version of the Joseph story, but I will not preach any more of them. I do believe in the simply perfect words of Julian of Norwich that "All shall be well, and all shall be well, and all manner of thing shall be well." But eschatology, the vision of time's end, is not an excuse to avoid ethics in the here and now.

The font of my father's baptism is not unalloyed bronze. It is a well of grace, brimming with what Heschel called the pathos of God. It is also the desert pit where the church betrayed and sold our sisters and brothers for blood money. I see both. They do not match. They do not resolve. I live in the paradox. The well runs dry. Streams flow in the desert. The water parts, and I hear the sound of silent weeping.

* * *

Jews have often done a better job than Christians when it comes to renouncing evil at the font. Despite the pressures of anti-Semitism, many Jews held back from baptism. During the Crusades, there were countless Jews who chose self-immolation over baptism: "It was so widespread that, as a scholar noted, 'even the worthless among us sacrifice themselves for the sake of *kiddush hashem*, and hardly one in a thousand turns apostate.'" Later, during the Spanish Inquisition, Jews, as well as Muslims, were killed or expelled for resisting conversion.

During the Third Reich, there were also many Jews who had no choice regarding baptism and conversion. Hundreds of Jewish children were able to survive because they were taken in by Church institutions and individuals. Many of these children were baptized without their families' permission. If this were simply a necessary survival tactic, the children would naturally have been returned to their communities following the war. Instead, a 1946 directive from the Vatican stated that, "Children who have been baptized must not be entrusted to institutions that would not be in a position to guarantee their Christian upbringing." Even orphaned children who had not been baptized were impacted: "For children who no longer have their parents, given the fact that the church has responsibility for them, it is not acceptable for them to be abandoned by the church or entrusted to any persons who have no rights over them." The Jewish community was considered as having no rights regarding these Jewish orphans. There was a chilling precedent for this position. In 1858, a six-year-old Jewish child was secretly baptized by a Roman Catholic maid in Bologna. Papal guards swept in and removed the little boy from his family.

Today Jews who were martyred for resisting conversion are honored with the title *Kedoshim*, holy ones. I, too, find their courageous witness worthy of honor. Does that mean that I find my grandparents' choice to be dishonorable? It is not my right to pass judgment upon them. In many ways, their choices are responsible for privileges that I have enjoyed. Their judgment sent my father across the waters to these shores and gave me life. At the same time, the knowledge of my Jewish roots challenges my understanding of my own baptismal identity. Were it not for centuries of anti-Semitism, I am convinced that my grandparents would never have made their way to that font. My father would have had his *bris* but no baptism. He would have studied for his bar mitzvah rather than his confirmation. I might be a rabbi rather than a Lutheran pastor—(or more likely, I would not have been, period). But of course, it's impossible to reverse the trajectory of history. The *tallit* my father might have worn was torn to shreds like Joseph's coat.

I do believe that my grandparents approached the font with hope and that their hope was both like and unlike my own. They hoped for their children's lives and futures. In the waters of baptism, my husband and I sought life beyond what we could secure for our children on our own, as did my grandparents. They turned to the church for the sake of their children and their children's children. In a way, for me and for my children. Our trip to the font with each child began with my grandparents' steps there. I remember how we carefully dressed each baby in the white lace gown handed down from my maternal great-grandmother, fastening the tiny pearl buttons. My mother came from New Jersey for each baptism and spent the night and made sure that the dress was perfectly ironed and ready to go. She had worn the same baptismal gown and so had I. We missed my father. We missed him often, but especially at such significant times. According to my mother, he was the one who urged her to hasten my baptism because he was more actively involved with his faith at that time than she was. He died six years before Ana's birth. We baptized her on Holy Cross Day when she was two months old. Three years later, when Hans was the same age, Ana stood on tip-toe to see the water wash over her baby brother. She watched the lighting of his baptismal candle. Then she turned and lifted up her dress, as three-year-olds sometimes do.

It is devastating to imagine that my faith may have cost my grandparents theirs, that my faith is bound to their trauma and terror. In the end, the temporal protection my grandparents sought proved illusory. On December 17, 1941, St. Mary's was draped with Nazi flags, and all baptisms of Jews, including my father's, were declared to be invalid.

KNIT TOGETHER

You are the one who created my innermost parts;
  you knit me together while I was still in my mother's womb.
I give thanks to you that I was marvelously set apart.
  Your works are wonderful—I know that very well.

—Psalm 139:13-14

As I began to share some of my new discoveries with friends and congregants in New York, I received a variety of responses. The ones that surprised me most were: "You won't like us any more!" from a few, worried young German families who bring their children to Wee Worship; "You seem so open to having Jewish roots!" from several Jews who expected me to be unhappy to discover this heritage; and last but not least, "Are you going to become Jewish now?" One person in my congregation put it more personally, "Are you going to leave us to become a rabbi?" I think of the transgender youth in our shelter who feel that they have been born in the wrong body. I suppose that I could feel trapped inside the wrong religion, except that I don't. At least, I usually don't. I have moments, when I light the silver candlesticks from my father's trunks and see the Jews of the Upper West Side, my neighbors, spilling out onto the sidewalks on their way to Shabbat services, and I imagine being among them. I have moments, like the unexpectedly tearful visit to the Jewish deli on a Friday afternoon. I want to say, "Things are not as they appear. I belong to you too!" but who would accept that? I hesitate to even share such longings for fear that they will make no sense to Jews or to Christians, but as Pascal wrote of love, "the heart has reasons that reason cannot know."

I have always been very drawn to Judaism, which I studied in college with the Jewish scholar Jacob Neusner. As a child in Sunday school, what we called the "Old Testament" stories were usually much more engaging to me than most anything we were presented with from the New Testament. Every year, we began with Jesus saying "let the children come to me." This was nice, but it was also boring. The children on Jesus' lap just sat there. The children of the Hebrew Scriptures got to do stuff. They were more fun. Daniel went in the lions' den. David had all kinds of extracurricular activities. He took care of sheep, played his harp, wrote psalms, and went after Goliath. A giant! There were none of those in the New Testament. Samuel heard God speaking to him in the night. Then there was the whole Joseph saga with outsized sibling rivalry and fantastic coloring opportunities—the dreams with wheat, sun, stars, fat cows, skinny cows, and the wonderful coat of many colors.

It didn't escape my notice that other than those sitting on Jesus' lap, almost all the children in the New Testament were sick or dead.

The only exception was a boy who shared his lunch. Jesus made children healthy, but it just wasn't terribly exciting. I was interested in stories of girls who did more than sit passively or lie sick or dead and then get up. There are not many girl stories in the Hebrew Scriptures either, but the ones we learned about featured real heroines. Moses' sister hides in the reeds, watching over her baby brother. When Pharaoh's daughter comes to take the baby, little Miriam bravely approaches her (a princess!) and does what it takes so that that Moses' own mother can nurse him. Then there was the girl who told General Naaman how to find healing for his leprosy through the prophet Elisha. She may have been young and a servant, but she knew vital things that the decorated general did not. These girls didn't lie down as something was done to them. They acted. They took charge. They did things that mattered, life and death things that seemed more important and daring than a boy handing over his fish sandwich when the adults asked for it.

Even the animals in the Hebrew Scriptures were more interesting. In seminary, I learned that the story of Noah's ark is not age appropriate for young children. Fortunately, my Sunday school teacher had not heard this. Despite the cataclysmic side of the story, what child does not like to play with the animals and line up them up, if one were lucky enough to have a model ark, or at least, to draw them? Then there was a talking donkey. None of the New Testament donkeys had anything to say. And, of course, there was the whale, the great whale that swallows Jonah alive and vomits him out. Whales and throw-up, what child would snooze through that?

The call of Jesus' disciples was dull compared with the call story of Jonah. Jesus walked along the beach and called the fisherman to follow. They left their nets and did. No drama. No large animals. Not even a burning bush. The bush got Moses' attention, and it got mine. We were even allowed to use glitter when we colored it. We left the classroom, like Moses coming down the mountain, with sparkling faces and glittery hair.

I could go on, but from my child's vantage point, the world of the New Testament was somewhat flat compared with the thrilling, vibrant world of the Hebrew Scriptures. The New Testament had its miracles and, of course, there was Christmas which was so good that it almost made up for everything else. Palm Sunday, Easter, and Pentecost were good, too. What's more dramatic than rising from the dead? As a child, I could have given a long answer. The flames and tongues of Pentecost were exciting too, but that was just one day. Even today, I find myself preaching from the Hebrew Scriptures, my first love, as often as from the New Testament.

The Christianity that I embrace does not seek to convert Jews. It does not blame Jews for the crucifixion of Jesus. I believe that Jesus died at Roman hands precisely because he resisted, with every fiber of his being, the demonizing and dehumanizing of anyone. We are divided, but in so many ways we are knit together. We share scripture, we claim the same ancestors of faith, we share the same prayer book of one hundred and fifty psalms that many of us pray daily.

Every year, on the night before Easter, many churches celebrate a vigil. We begin in darkness and light a fire outside from which we light the candles we carry into the church where we gather to hear stories. The stories we tell on the threshold of Easter are all tales of life surprising people in the face of death. Often, our children and youth act them out. The dry bones envisioned by the prophet Ezekiel get up and dance around the church. King Nebuchadnezzar commands his people to bow before the golden statue he has erected while sporting an enormous diamond-encrusted dollar-sign necklace. Shadrach, Meshach, and Abednego refuse to reverence the idol and go defiantly into the flames of the fiery furnace that they've painted red and orange the week before. Jonah slides out from the giant mouth of a paper whale across the floor and heads off to Nineveh, next to the piano. The wicked people of Nineveh are played by nine-year-old girls. "You make me sick!" "You make me sicker!" "I hate you!" "I hate you more!" "Stop copying me!" "Stop copying *me!*" They have improvised the script themselves. "Stop it!" says Jonah. "God loves you." The girls grin and give each other high fives. If only it were so easy, but they are learning the stories and making them their own. This is what we hope for because these stories are our lifelines, and these are all Jewish stories that we teach our children.

How are we linked to these stories? Ironically, it happens through the storied waters of baptism. We believe that in baptism our lives are joined to Jesus in every way and that his Jewish heritage becomes our own. We claim the same lineage, the same matriarchs and patriarchs as family. And so in baptism, I was already intimately connected to my Jewish heritage, and I wonder how it is now different. Yet it is. Although baptism ties us together, it is also there that we part company over our differing view of Jesus, there that, at moments, my own heart is torn in two.

Although the rites of baptism and Holy Communion have been a source of division, they also point to a shared understanding among Christians and Jews, the belief that matter matters.

For Christians, the mattering of matter is at the heart of the incarnation, the Word made flesh. In baptism and Communion, we take material things—water, bread and wine. We wash, we eat, we drink and find ourselves shaken awake by a holy visitation like Jacob in the Bible who wipes the sleep from his eyes one morning and sees that the stone pillow beneath his head is the gate of heaven.

Where do we get this notion of washing, eating, and drinking as portals of divinity? It comes to us from deep within the Jewish experience. Jews have a code for daily, consistent actions and blessings covering virtually all aspects of life in order to remember this, something that Christians often fail to do; yet we share belief in a God who is both transcendent and immanent, beyond us and with us. We are knit together, but for 2000 years Christians have broken faith with our Jewish siblings in the most egregious ways.

* * *

How can I embrace a faith as life-giving when it has crushed out so much life? One might ask this of any number of religions. There is no major world religion with clean hands, including Judaism, perhaps only Jainism. But Christians bear a unique burden in relationship to Jews. As a descendant of Jews who suffered and died in the Shoah, how can I unreservedly find my identity at the font? I have been confounded by the violent history of Christianity before, but now this issue has become far more intimate, pounding through my heart like blood. Uli was correct in saying it is "terribly complex."

This complexity has historical antecedents. Why would a slave adopt the religion of his oppressors? Assimilation wasn't even on the table. In 1667, a law made clear that no slave would be exempt from bondage just because they had been baptized. Why would there even be a church in Latin America, given the atrocities of the conquistadores? Bartolomé de las Casas wrote a scathing account of these crimes committed against the indigenous peoples of Latin America.

In the face of European denial, he documented the seizing of land and property, enslavement, torture and the genocide of native people, making a mockery of baptism itself:

> As the Spanish wretches went about with their savage dogs trying to terrorize the Indians, men and women alike, one woman (thinking to soften the hearts of the Spaniards) tied her year-old child to her foot and hanged herself from a beam. No sooner had she done this than the dogs arrived and tore her child to pieces. It must be added that a Franciscan friar baptized the child before it died.

De las Casas cites numerous incidents of children literally being thrown to the dogs. One tribal chief was being preached at while tied to a stake. He was told that he should convert so that he could go to heaven when he died. He asked where he would go if he didn't convert and was told that he would go to hell and suffer eternal torment. He then asked if all Christians went to heaven. When told that they did, he replied that he would prefer to go to hell.

In spite of what de las Casas called "the Devastation of the Indies" and other devastations at Spanish hands, today in most parts of Latin America, Roman Catholicism is the dominant faith, certainly Christianity. Latin Americans ultimately found a source of solace and solidarity in the sufferings of Jesus. I saw a crucifix in Mexico, covered with painted drops of blood, except for the feet where people could reach and touch. The feet and ankles have been worn down to their wooden bones from all the touching. It is a place of connection. This is the discovery of the hymns called spirituals—"Nobody knows the trouble I've seen, nobody knows but Jesus." Latino, African American, Womanist, Mujerista, and queer theologians have all given voice to theologies of liberation, rather than oppression. One could argue that the religion adopted is not the same religion of conquerors or slave holders, but a purer version of the faith that had been corrupted, usurping the name "Christianity" for what was actually an idol formed in the image of human hatreds and prejudices.

This idolatrous "Christianity" lives on. It sanctifies racism and militarism, bigotry and greed packaged as holy prosperity. It drives gay, lesbian, bisexual and transgender youth to self-hatred and suicide. Too many young people have sat in my office and told me their fears of going to hell. One gay teen was told that unless he "converted" to heterosexuality, he would spend eternity in hell with demons pouring hot oil over him and that his nerve endings would remain undamaged to make sure he felt the endless agony, a little detail seen to by the devil. Plenty of adults who have suffered a version of this abusive vitriol refuse to have anything to do with the church. Others who have been burned to the core continue to find their way back. In my congregation, some of them not only attend but serve in positions of strong, compassionate leadership. It is an awesome mystery that such goodness can spring free from the very maws of evil.

✳ ✳ ✳

My grandparents could have clung to their Jewish faith in the face of evil. Because they did not, out of that terrible loss, I received a different gift of faith. How can I claim something good for myself out of that carnage? I know that for some, my arrival at the font can never be viewed as something good. Instead, it would be better if I were Jewish because it would be better if my grandparents had not felt any pressure to baptize their children. I wholeheartedly agree with the

The memorial in the rathaus (city hall) of the murdered senators, including my grandfather.

The memorial for the synagogue that stood in Wittmund where my grandfather grew up.

A family tombstone in Wittmund for Samson Aron Neumark

Wittmund memorial

Edzard and Carsten

Neumark Family Wittmund

The villa (where my father grew up, built by my grandfather).

Klaus

Four Brothers Neumark Wittmund (ca. 1865)

My Aunt Susy (mother of Peter, Ursula, and Klaus).

Aunt Lore in 1932.

Aunt Lore, Christmas 1943, a month before my grandparents were deported.

My grandfather, Moritz Neumark.

My father soon after he came to the US in his US army uniform.

Me with Oma (1955).

My mother, me (at 18 months old), and Oma. This was my first time visiting my grandmother in Switzerland in 1955.

My father with Oma (his mother).

The street in Theresienstadt where my grandparents were imprisoned.

The house where they were taken (60 held per room).

The windowsill of the same house (where I left a rose).

Oma and Peter (my cousin).

Theresienstadt Crematoriam.

Oma in Switzerland.

My parents and me, 1959.

The street in Wittmund where my grandfather grew up

latter, but I am who I am. I used to have trouble praying the line in Psalm 139 about being a wonderful work. I didn't feel wonderfully made, but with time has come the grace of self-acceptance.

Now, in this time, the self I am is not quite the self I thought I was. I thought my Christian identity came through a long, un-interrupted line of baptisms. To consider that my faith is aligned with a Jewish lineage severed by anti-Semitic savagery and evil is soul-wrenching. I grieve for this loss of Jewish identity, but I do not regret the faith that has guided, gladdened, and sustained me, even though the center of my joy is seared with lament. Faith mattered deeply to my Jewish forebears and to my parents, to my father. I find myself held in the continuity of their love of God and caught in a heartbreaking divide. I believe God is caught there too.

The oldest thing that survived the wartime wreckage of St. Mary's is not the bronze font. It is God's love. In *mikvah* or font, we are bathed in love we can only imagine, if it all, through a glass, darkly.

TOTENTANZ

Among the many works of art destroyed in the firebombing of St. Mary's was a painted frieze that depicted a common medieval theme, the dance of death or *Totentanz*. In the painting, death dances with representative figures from pope to peasant and, finally, an infant in her cradle. The post-war restoration of St. Mary's includes a stained-glass window patterned after the lost painting. One of the citizens snatched away in Lübeck's perverse *Totentanz* was my grand-father. His wife and children were caught up as well, though each of them was able to slip free. On January 30, 1933, Hitler was appointed chancellor and sworn into power. Immediately, my grandfather was forced to vacate the numerous positions of civic and industrial leadership he'd held for years, including his position on the executive committee of the Reich Association of German Industry.

This board, which had included a number of Jews, was disbanded and reformed. Hitler appointed Gustav Krupp as the sole director. Krupp had already invested millions of his family's steel fortune into Hitler's election, seduced by the prospect of a de-unionized labor force, and he persuaded many fellow industrialists to make similar contributions. Fritz Thyssen, a friend who had once invited my grandfather to several of his board memberships, now fully supported the exclusion of Jews from German industry and was himself a key financier of the Nazi war machine.

It all came as a shock, even though my grandfather must have been politically aware given his position on the senate, among others. Nevertheless, just three years earlier, in 1930, even as Hitler's influence grew, my grandfather received a public affirmation of his many contributions—an honorary doctorate from the University of Aachen. The honor was bestowed even though his Jewish background was not a secret. My grandfather may have baptized his children and even considered himself to be Lutheran, but he continued to do business with Jews, to socialize with Jews, and to run a business supported, in large part, by Jewish investors. For him, Jewish ties, German identity, and civic engagement all fit together. There was, however, no room for such a mix in the National Socialist platform under Hitler.

Only three months after Hitler's rise to power, in a letter dated April 29, 1933, my grandfather penned his response to Hermann Fabry, the chairman of the iron works board and an old friend. He and his wife ate at my grandparents' table, and he enjoyed hunting with my grandfather. Now Fabry was evidently pressuring him to resign in light of the coming "Ayranization" of the German economy, including the removal of Jews from positions of German industrial prominence. I received a copy of the handwritten letter from Jan Lokers, the director of Lübeck's archives, where the original resides. The letter, including its fierce exclamation points, fills me with pride and profound sadness. It reads, in part:

Dear Mr. Fabry!

My thanks for your advice of yesterday. At the beginning of the unfortunate last revolution, Kaiser Wilhelm's loyal assistants and generals advised him to abandon his duties and go to Holland. In hindsight, all German-feeling people disapproved of this action and some went as far as to call the old Kaiser a deserter.

You know my background and my German convictions . . . I will never leave my post as a coward! I was a soldier and I defended my conception of life with tenacity, all my life long. If hard work and self-sacrificing devotion do not count in the new Germany, we should not disguise that anymore. I will not desert voluntarily, but only give way to force!

This is my position upon which I will stand with my rights and my good, *German* conscience. How far my old friends will follow me must be left to them individually. After my hardworking life, I will not now waste away the short remaining years.

I will be back on Tuesday. Kindly let the office know about my return. I thank you again for your amicable suggestions and send my best greetings to you and your wife,

Your devoted,

Neumark.

It must have seemed to my grandfather that his words were powerless and that his stand for truth in the face of deceit meant nothing; but eighty years later, thanks to a city archivist who spent hours going through hundreds of pages of papers, my grandfather's letter came into my hands. Now, his words break open my heart and inspire me daily to keep faith at times when critical efforts appear to be futile.

You never know when your witness will break through. Recently, a two-thousand-year-old seed for an extinct date palm tree was found in an archeological site in Israel. Some scientists planted it and the ancient seed sprouted and produced a new tree, unfurling shiny leaves in the startled sun. For me, my grandfather's letter carries the prophetic power of Isaiah's words:

> Just as the rain and the snow come down from the sky
> > and don't return there without watering the earth,
> > making it conceive and yield plants
> > and providing seed to the sower and food to the eater,
> > so is my word that comes from my mouth;
> > it does not return to me empty. (Isaiah 55:10-11a)

Less than a year after he wrote the letter, my grandfather, despite his "good *German* conscience" was forcibly removed from the iron works. He was a visible sign of the "Jewification" of the German economy. A known Jew could not remain as the head of Lübeck's largest employer. An internal paper from the Lübeck senate, where my grandfather had so recently served, stated that he was forbidden to go to the company for any reason. The paper was dated September 17, 1934, seventeen months after my grandfather's own "Here I stand" resolution.

Fritz Thyssen, one of the "old friends" mentioned in the letter, was offered the chance to seize the iron works but declined. I wonder if some shred of human feeling prevented him from doing it. He later repudiated the violence of *Kristallnacht* and resigned his Nazi party membership. He paid for his infidelity to the Reich as a traitor in Dachau, but some question whether Hitler's campaign would ever have gotten off the ground successfully without the enormous influx of wealth that Thyssen provided back when he and Krupp saluted Hitler as an economic savior. Krupp remained an avid Nazi, and his empire expanded further with each German invasion. He was able to build factories in occupied countries and use the slave labor supplied by concentration camps. Krupp even ran one of his factories inside Auschwitz. Thyssen, Krupp, and their fortunes survived the war, and Krupp was relieved of his war crimes' trial because of advanced dementia.

Now, Fritz Thyssen and Gustav Krupp have been dogging my heels because of their booming elevator and escalator business. I am reminded of them and their blood-soaked empires every time I step into a ThyssenKrupp elevator or onto a ThyssenKrupp escalator. If I go across the street into the housing project and get in the elevator to take Communion to a homebound member or to visit a single mom with four children to talk about their baptism, I see their names. If I ride the escalator up to the elevators at the Memorial Sloan-Kettering Cancer Center to read the Bible and pray with a woman dying of cancer, I bump into Fritz and Gustav. Living in space-starved Manhattan, many stores have multiple levels reached by escalators. Need a hoodie at Modell's? Fritz and Gustav got there first. Cat food at Petco? There they are. I can't even walk around the corner to the supermarket to get a gallon of milk or a dozen eggs without running into them. I never noticed this before, but now, each time, I feel a pang of fury and sorrow.

✳ ✳ ✳

In a strange twist, my father was permitted to stay on running the iron works copper production until 1938. Jan Lokers, the archivist, told me that this was extremely surprising. It required not only the decision of the new owners, but the Nazis had to approve it as well. The senate Nazis conducted an investigation of my father and determined that because he was not engaged in any political-resistance activities, they would allow him to stay. It was likely that they lacked a ready replacement and needed his expertise to keep things running smoothly. Since his role at the firm was less notable, he could remain under the radar for the time being. It might seem odd for my father to agree to work at the iron works after his father was kicked out, but Klaus told me that Moritz was happy about it and urged my father to stay. It was extremely difficult for my grandfather to let go of his life work and to accept that his ouster was permanent. Having his son there on a daily basis allowed him to retain a sense of connection and even some control.

According to the official version of events, my grandfather had retired. A newspaper article quoted Fabry as wishing him *einen schönen Lebensabend*—a lovely evening of life. Shortly afterward, the firm was bought by the Flick Concern, owned and run by Frederick Flick (1883–1972). After the war, Flick would be convicted of war crimes that including taking over the iron works. The charges against him at the Nuremburg trial included forcing Jews to transfer their property to non-Jews and the enslavement of laborers "on a gigantic scale," using war prisoners and concentration camp inmates in manu-facturing work. The iron works quickly became a key industrial player in the Jew-killing machine run by prisoners of war. In their closing arguments, Flick claimed that he and his co-defendants were being persecuted for their entrepreneurial business acumen.

After the war, Marshall Plan funds helped to repair minor dam-age wrought by Allied bombings and the iron works prospered for a time. Flick eventually sold it, and in 1975 it was bought by U.S. Steel for thirty million marks. Their planned revival of the business failed. It was sold for two marks in 1978 and demolished. All that remains today are the museum and the villa.

* * *

When my grandparents were removed from the iron works, they also had to leave the grand home my grandfather designed and had built, since it was considered to be property of the firm. They moved into what Renate described as a small but nice home in an-other area of the city. I hired a taxi and gave the driver the address I had found in the archives. As we chatted, he mentioned that his own father had worked at the iron works in the 1960s and early 1970s. We arrived at the house, no grand villa with space for garden parties, but nevertheless, a fine home overlooking a park across the street. They rented because there was always the hope of returning to their rightful place. I have a photo of my grandparents out for a stroll in the park. They had it turned into a postcard. They appear as they were, a well-turned out couple, walking together, he in a jaunty hat, she with white-gloved hands holding a black purse and a thin cane, giving their best faces to the camera. Klaus recalled that after the move, Moritz began to spend a huge amount of time playing tennis: "He lost himself in tennis."

My father had already moved into the apartments that the iron works built for management. His sister Susy had married and moved to Berlin. The youngest, Lore, remained at home with her parents. Their time in the new house was short-lived. Renate told us that friends cautioned my grandparents against staying in Lübeck where they were so well known. It would be advisable to relocate to Berlin where they could more easily disappear from official state attention.

In 1936, my grandparents said goodbye to the city where they had raised their children and built their lives and moved to Berlin. In remembering it, Renate couldn't stop from repeating the obvious: "It was so bitter to leave everything. . . . They never believed it would happen. . . . It was very difficult to leave." My grandfather's heart was broken long before it actually stopped beating.

THE BELLS OF ST. MARY'S

Many people can recall *The Bells of St. Mary's*, the sentimental 1945 film starring Bing Crosby and Ingrid Bergman as the priest and nun who preside over a church crisis that resolves to the tearful satisfaction of all within two hours. Among numerous nominations, the film won an Academy Award for Best Sound. For me, the bells of St. Mary's signify the sound of silence. They rang for the last time while battered by wind gusts during the firestorm of bombs that struck St. Mary's cathedral in Lübeck in 1942. Their remains were found at the base of the church's south tower—a heap of bronze wreckage, the bells cracked apart and warped from the fire, the stone floor buckled and crushed under their weight. When the rest of the cathedral was restored, the broken bells were left untouched, and they lie there still with their twisted, rusty tongues.

* * *

I don't remember much about the trip my parents and I took to Lübeck when I was eight, but I do remember our visit to St. Mary's. I remember being stopped by the disturbing scene behind an iron gate set across a whitewashed brick alcove in the back of the church. How strange that the bells' breakage had not been carted away or pieced back together and that even the dirt around them had not been swept clean. In the perfect, gothic geometry of this cathedral, I was mesmerized by the one thing that did not belong, a pile of mis-shapen, ugly metal.

I think the broken bells captured my attention so profoundly be-cause the Lutheran churches of my childhood were oddly sanitized spaces. Our well-kept sanctuary disdained Jesus' crucified body on a cross. For one thing, such displays were considered too Roman Cath-olic. Jesus' suffering was a thing of the past. He was now ascended to heaven and did not drip blood in our very clean churches. When we were presented with Holy Communion, Christ's body came as an ane-mic white circle stamped with an empty cross. Christ's blood was Gallo wine poured into one-sip-sized, individual glasses that were quickly whisked away on a special silver tray to be washed immediately after services. I know this because my mother was a member of the altar guild and when she washed—always in very hot, soapy water, I dried. (of course, I had to scrub my own hands first!). Germs had no chance.

Looking back, I see the unfortunate, subliminal message that if material messiness was not welcome in our church, what of the disordered corners of our own lives? What about our violence-prone, bloodied world? Well, we covered that in a short, generic, confession of sin and moved on. I remember a Lutheran bishop who liked to say that Jesus didn't die on a golden cross between two candlesticks, but for me, the cross had become such a familiar object, that it lost the power to shock. Perhaps the same would have been true of a crucifix. On the other hand, the broken bells were something I'd never seen before, and they commanded attention. It was the same for our son, Hans. When he was eight-years-old and we visited St. Mary's with my mother, Hans had eyes for nothing but the ruined bells. Whenever I tried to direct his attention to other sights in the vast cathedral, he was drawn back by their awful, magnetic power. Even to a young child it was clear that something bad had happened here. But what was it about? There is little explication of the powerful scene, only that the cathedral was bombed in an act of wartime retaliation. The church is portrayed as a victim.

* * *

The congregation of my early childhood changed radically during my teen years. Race relations, space travel, world hunger, nuclear war, and medical ethics were typical topics of the forums that followed worship, as theology pushed us into the world, not away from it. The cross above the altar remained empty, but a new artwork was commissioned by our pastor in honor of his wife who was dying of cancer. It was an exacting reproduction of the bottom section from Lucas Cranach the Elder's 1547 Wittenberg altarpiece, which depicts Luther in the pulpit preaching while pointing to Christ on the cross. It was given a place of honor on the wall of our sanctuary.

I loved the coming together of word and image in this painting because what we say about the cross makes all the difference. Words can pervert the cross into a swastika that demonizes Jews as Christ-killers. Words can co-opt the cross for an agenda of hate and a model for masochism, urging people to bear their cross of abuse, poverty, or slavery. Words can crucify the bodies of women and children. But for many, the opposite is true. The cross can point to the defiance of oppression and can be a sign of justice-loving, rather than self-hating, martyrdom. Dietrich Bonhoeffer embodied his words as he joined the plot to murder Hitler: "When Christ calls a man, he bids him come and die." For many others, exemplified by those whose reverent touch had worn the painted blood from Jesus' feet in a Mexican crucifix, the cross is a source of comfort, a sign of God's solidarity on the margins. Jesus' cry from the cross, "My God, My God, why have you abandoned me?" is at once a scream of absence and a prayer that somehow assumes presence, using the words of Psalm 22. There, where God feels most absent, God is present.

* * *

As little acquainted with direct suffering as I was in my childhood, I absorbed the images of concentration camps shown in school, the pictures of starving children offered at church, and TV footage from the My Lai massacre and race riots in nearby Newark. This was not the world as it was supposed to be, and I was the kind of child who lay awake for hours aching and puzzling over such things. When the leader of a drug-rehab program for teens spoke with our church youth group and invited anyone to come to visit them "even if you don't have a drug problem," I decided to take him up on it. I wanted to better understand another suffering of my time— the grip of addiction on so many lives.

Against their better judgment, my parents dutifully drove me to the storefront. I stepped into what looked like a head shop, with thick incense and psychedelic, antiwar posters tacked over the Indian-print bedspreads on the walls. (I was well acquainted with the vibe of head shops since they had the best selection of anti-war buttons in town.) So far, so cool. Then to my great surprise, I was handed a cup and told to go pee in it. I explained that this was not necessary since I was just taking up their leader on his invitation to attend "even if you don't have a drug problem." The guy with the cup regarded me with jaded eyes and made it clear that my pee was the price of entry. I soon learned that no one there accepted my sincere interest, but I stuck out my mission to educate myself even as they began a campaign to coax the truth out of me.

About a month after my first visit, I found myself sitting in a circle on the grungy carpet where we were meant to share how our drug use had screwed up our lives and ineffectively tried to numb our pain. As devastating stories moved around the circle, closing in on me like a shiver of sharks, I had no idea what to say. I wracked my brain for something, anything that I could throw out to assuage their hunger, but there was nothing. I had never stolen and sold my mother's inherited jewelry to buy drugs. I had never given blow jobs for extra cash to the dad who drove me home from babysitting. I did not live with an evil, perverted stepfather. In fact, I had never even inhaled. After listening to the girl sitting beside me recount the night she was gang-raped on an old couch in her ex-boyfriend's suburban basement, I was speechless. I felt too paralyzed to get up and leave. I had gone there to learn but was now an involuntary voyeur and target. All eyes were on me. I was their main project— break this girl down so that she'll give up her dirty secrets at last. They went from gentle urgings to full-out yelling at me to come clean for my own good.

I left in tears, the bearer only of a deep, inherited secret that even I did not know existed. When I got into the car, my parents immediately saw how upset I was, despite my efforts to hide it. They were primed to forbid my further participation, but I had already decided for myself that the days of peeing my way into the underside of suburban adolescence had come to an end. Also, why was I so lucky when these peers of mine had been so badly hurt? Why was God so unfair? Like many before and after, I could no longer believe in a God who refused to intervene and end the suffering here, there, and everywhere.

A weird parasite challenged my disbelief. I became host to a hoard of miniscule *Toxoplasma gondii* after eating beefsteak tartar, raw beef, with my parents. At that time, toxoplasmosis was only familiar to veterinarians who treated cows. Fortunately, our next-door neighbor was a world-class parasitologist, and he led us to the specialist who would correctly diagnosis and treat me. But that took two long years, and in the meantime, it looked like I was going to die. I didn't want to. The universe might not be all it was supposed to be, but there was more than enough that held me here. My body remained listless, but I was jolted with a fierce longing to live and to multiply good in the face of everything that attacked it. In that desire, I gradually experienced the mysterious yet undeniable pull of God. In the case of the prophet Jonah, God appointed a worm to direct him back on his prophetic path. In my case, it was an invading swarm of little protozoan.

At first, my newfound faith was a holy blur. Later, it was the strange lens of the cross and Martin Luther's words about it that brought things into focus and led me back to the Lutheran church. Luther's theology of the cross rejects God-talk that refers only to things that make sense and offer ready answers. "It is living, no rather dying, suffering and facing damnation, not thinking, reading and speculating that makes a theologian," said Luther. This connected with my own experience. Luther's sense of God's hidden-ness both in and behind suffering also seems strikingly Jewish. Abraham Heschel wrote, "To celebrate is to invoke God's presence concealed in God's absence."

Luther was a scholar of the Hebrew scriptures, and he was drawn to the Hebrew concept of *Hester Panim*, the hiding of the divine face. He related our inability to see God clearly to Moses' seeing only the backside or hindparts of God. As a Christian, Luther also describes Joseph and Mary wiping Jesus' hindparts and changing his dirty diapers, glory hidden in the thick of excrement and later, executed on a garbage dump. As Jesus was crucified, the gospels report that "It was now about noon, and darkness covered the whole earth until about three o'clock"(Luke 23:44). God was murdered, and the light of the world is extinguished.

In *Night*, Eli Wiesel writes famously of God's death in Auschwitz.

> Never shall I forget that nocturnal silence which deprived me, for all eternity, of the desire to live. Never shall I forget those moments which murdered my God and my soul and turned my dreams to dust.

As Wiesel is forced to watch the hanging of another child, he hears someone behind him ask "Where is God? Where is He?" "I heard a voice within me answer him: 'Where is He? Here He is—He is hanging here on this gallows. . . . '"

There appears to be a kinship between God on the gallows and God on the cross, but instead, it tears us apart as the belief of one people was used to propel the genocide of another. Do Luther's words about the Jews cancel his many other words and their power for good? I would not read anything Hitler wrote and think, "This is fantastic, despite all the bad stuff he said."— and some of Luther's words are as vile as anything Hitler said. There is one key difference, however, which is that Hitler's hatred of Jews became central to everything he said and did. This was not the case with Luther. Our church has repented of the reformer's hateful words, but we should not forget them and their ghastly harvest. It is no longer possible for me to gaze at a painting of Luther preaching on the cross, however crucial much of his understanding has been for my own faith, without seeing the blood of millions of innocent Jews. It is another painting that speaks to me now, the work of a Jewish artist.

In 1938, Marc Chagall painted *The White Crucifixion*. An unmistakably Jewish Jesus hangs from a cross, wearing a *tallit* around his waist. The halo over his head is reflected in the halo of light circling the menorah beneath him. The crucified one is surrounded by images of Nazi persecution set against a cold, snowy background. We see a village visited by the kind of pogrom that savaged Germany in November of that year. Flames shoot from the windows of toppling houses and from a pillaged synagogue. One Torah scroll unrolls in the snow as a man clasps another to his chest trying to flee. He runs beside a boat of refugees that is already full. A mother clutching her baby disappears at the bottom of the painting. In the smoky sky above the cross, three Biblical patriarchs and a matriarch

appear to reach their hands out in despair, mouths agape in horror. The woman is Rachel, "crying for her children; she refuses to
be consoled, because her children are no more" (Jeremiah 31:15b).
Chagall's painting offers no hint of redemption. Jesus is not depicted
as anyone's savior, just as one more slaughtered Jew. What does this
mean for those who do claim Jesus as their savior? It convicts us and
challenges us to recognize Jesus himself as a victim of the church,
along with so many others.

A year before he completed this painting, Chagall had already
been condemned by the Nazis as a producer of "Degenerate Art."
The White Crucifixion was shown in Paris in 1940, and soon afterward Chagall escaped to the United States until the end of the war.
In 1944, he wrote

> . . . after two thousand years of "Christianity" in the world—
> say whatever you like—but, with few exceptions, their hearts
> are silent... I see the artists in Christian nations sit still—who
> has heard them speak up? They are not worried about them-
> selves, and our Jewish life doesn't concern them.

For me, the silent bells of Lübeck recall the cracking apart of
Christian moral authority that occurred in St. Mary's, a cathedral
where the Aryanization of the German church joined the Aryanization of German industry. Just as the Nazis sought to determine the
racial make-up of Germans in order to rid "the fatherland" of Jews,
church leaders in Lübeck were prominent among those mobilizing to
cleanse congregations, scriptures, worship materials, and Jesus himself from any trace of Jewish blood. There was no solace to be had in
church as my grandparents' world came apart since the church was
part of their undoing.

* * *

Hitler pandered to the anti-Semitism that was already rooted in the German church. Early in 1933, two days after opening a Reichstag meeting from a church lectern, Hitler announced that churches would be "pillars of the Third Reich." Party members were urged to participate in the religious side of German culture and tradition. This manipulative nod from the Führer was all that many church leaders needed to hear. Catholic bishops withdrew their prohibition against joining the Nazi party, and many Protestant leaders embraced Hitler's vision of a united German church whose members were called German Christians.

The role of Jewish converts quickly became a central question since churches had always understood membership to be founded in baptism rather than ethnicity. Did Jews like my father lose their Jewishness in the waters of baptism? According to the German Christians, they did not. Already in 1932 the baptism of Jewish converts was viewed as "the gateway for alien blood to enter the body of our nation." Or even more crudely, "Just as a pig remains a pig, even if you put it in a horse's stall, so a Jew still remains a Jew, even if he is baptized."

The beloved city of my father and grandparents harbored a radical wing of the German Christian movement. In 1934 Bishop Erwin Balzer came to St. Mary's. He was only thirty-three years old and a member of the Nazi party since 1931. In describing his beliefs, Balzer wrote: "My theological position is derived from the National Socialist ideology." The bishop worked quickly to attract like-minded clergy to Lübeck, installing pro-Nazi leaders in the place of others. There were small pockets of resistance. Early in his administration,

Balzer tried to remove a Jewish convert who had served as a volunteer Sunday School teacher at St. Mary's for many years. She was a beloved member of the community, and Balzer's attempt was blocked by her supporters. Balzer then narrowed his focus to ensure that church officials, pastors, and paid employees were demonstratively Aryan. He would deal with congregants in time.

* * *

The complicity of silence is bad enough, but the church was not silent. German Christians vocalized their hate with press releases and pamphlets rife with anti-Jewish propaganda in the weeks the led up to *Kristallnacht* in November of 1938. Two days before the pogrom, they held a conference characterizing Judaism as a dangerous religion. Immediately following *Kristallnacht*, another Nazi bishop responded with a pamphlet that reprinted Luther's most noxious writings against Jews. Soon afterward, Bishop Balzer joined a small collective that sought to bring the church even more closely into lock-step with the Nazis.

In the spring of 1939, this group launched the Eisenach Institute at the Wartburg Castle where Martin Luther hid following his excommunication and where he translated the New Testament into German. They wanted to present their work as an extension of Luther's reforms. Balzer was one of eleven church leaders to sign the Institute's founding documents. He also brought on Johannes Sievers, a high-ranking church functionary from Lübeck to chair the board and oversee its finances.

The Institute's purpose was to remove everything Jewish from the church's scripture, worship, teaching and life. The entire Old

Testament was scrapped, and all New Testament citations and references to the Hebrew Scriptures were eliminated. Jesus was Aryanized by a serpentine path concluding that his Galilean roots meant he could not have been Jewish. With a "purified" Bible, the Institute began its offensive against worship materials. Prayers from a posture of humble intercession or for forgiveness did not conform to the Nazi self-image. Men and women of the Reich were not subservient in any sphere, including the liturgical. Prayers were redirected to focus only on praise and acclamation. Hymns were scoured for references to the Old Testament, and even the word "Hallelujah" was banished.

Very few hymns survived intact, and this presented a problem that most pastors and rabbis are familiar with. People don't like their favorite hymns and worship music messed with. Not surprisingly, the new, Nazified hymnal did not catch on widely, although it was used at St. Mary's. In many other places, the pastoral approach was to pacify people with the old, nostalgic music while introducing butchered scriptures (sadly, it is just as likely today that congregants who might notice one word altered in a hymn would not recognize the mutilation of scripture) and increasingly anti-Jewish preaching. Sermons and catechisms needed a revamped Jesus:

> Today Jesus appears to us as the self-confident Lord in the best and highest sense of the word. It is his *life* which holds meaning for the German people, not his agonizing death . . . The mighty preacher and wrathful one in the temple . . . is the ideal which today shines forth from the Gospels, *not the sacrificial lamb of the Jewish prophets, not the crucified.*

Jesus emerged from the Institute as a strapping Aryan, a German saint who died as a hero fighting Judaism.

Some of the regional churches near Lübeck distanced themselves from the work of the Institute because they objected to the substantial gutting of familiar scriptures, prayers, and hymns. They also accepted the validity of Jewish conversion but made it clear that this did not include support for Jews. A spokesman for the church of Hamburg explained:

> Please understand my position against the Institute, which talks about the Jewish influence on church life . . . . The church has been the biggest opponent against Judaism, in the medieval times, before Luther and even until very recently. The church can have a clear conscience as it has always viewed Judaism as an opponent against all national life and has only stated one thing: The religious place of the Old Testament and the baptism of converted Jews have to remain. That has nothing to do with Jewish influence.

Although the hearty embrace met by the Institute in Lübeck was not the norm, neither was the Institute a fringe phenomenon. In addition to the anti-Semitic liturgical reformation it promoted, Institute leaders gave lectures and conferences attended by hundreds of German theologians. This theological pogrom provided a powerful basis for public violence. In one lecture, the head of the Institute, Siegfried Leffler, explained his position on genocide in 1936 even before it become official Nazi policy:

> As a Christian, I also have to follow the laws of my nation, . . . so that again I am brought into the harshest of conflicts with the Jews. Even if I know "thou shalt not kill" is a commandment of God or "thou shalt love the Jew" because he too is a child of the eternal Father, I am able to know as well that I

have to kill him, I have to shoot him and I can only do that if I am permitted to say: Christ.

As the Institute continued fomenting hate, Bishop Balzer advanced his local efforts to expel Jews, beginning to root out non-Aryan congregational members. He had the church constitution for Lübeck altered to officially state that "Jews cannot be members of the Evangelical Lutheran Church in Lübeck." Balzer was also more than happy to grant the Gestapo open access to church baptismal records in order to determine who had Jewish blood through Jewish parents or grandparents. Balzer was at the forefront of what would soon become law for the entire state church thanks to the influence of the Institute. On December 17, 1941, Balzer and the leaders of seven regional churches, issued a declaration that stated:

> As part of the German nation, the state churches and the church leaders stand on the forefront of the defense fight. It has become necessary to consider all Jews as born enemies of this world and nation and as Dr. Luther already demanded, to take severe actions against all Jews and to expel them from this country. Christian baptism does not change the race or the biological being of a Jew. A German Evangelical church has to look after the religious life of Germans. Christians with a Jewish origin do not have room nor right to take part in this life.

Even this did not go far enough for Balzer, who announced that the expulsion would be retroactive in Lübeck and all previous baptisms, such as those of my father and his sisters were declared to have been invalid. In reality, the December 17 statement had no impact on Lübeck's Jews, since the ninety who remained in the city in 1941 had been deported to Riga and murdered a month earlier. These included converts like Emma Grünfeldt, who had been teaching in Protestant schools for thirty years.

Thankfully, my father emigrated two and a half years before this deportation, and my grandparents had been settled in Berlin for nearly five years. Nevertheless, the city remained enshrined in their souls. How is it that one loves the place that has betrayed one to the point of death? How is it that my father found sanctuary in the very church that sought to exterminate him? It is a question that keeps plaguing me. The only thing I remember him ever saying about church in the thirties was listening to Helmut Thielicke preach.

Thielicke was a pastor and theologian in the Confessing Church, the only organized church resistance to the German Christians. Immediately following Hitler's blessing of a united Reich church, a group of Protestant clergy came together under the leadership of Swiss theologian Karl Barth and Lutheran pastor Martin Niemöller to oppose the German Christians. In April of 1934, Barth drafted the Barmen Declaration as the founding document for the Confessing Church, which grew to include about a fifth of German Protestants.

The Barmen Declaration decreed that the Bible is the sole source of divine revelation, Jesus Christ is Lord of all and has authority over all, and the state should not determine the forms of church life. Unlike the German Christians, the Confessing Church insisted on loyalty to Christ over Hitler and opposed the rejection of the Hebrew Scriptures and the imposition of the Aryan paragraph (which banned Jews from civil positions) for churches. Nothing in the Barmen Declaration mentions the Nazi persecution of Jews.

* * *

When I attended seminary in the late 1970 and early 80s, I remember learning about the Confessing Church as a singular Christian voice of challenge in the face of evil, and some Confessing Church members did wage a witness of resistance to Hitler; however, I was never taught how limited and flawed that witness was. It's understandable that Christians would want to find something to be proud of in the wake of overwhelming complicity and collaboration with the Nazis, but it's not excusable or helpful to whitewash the alarming truth.

Like all but the most rigidly controlled religious communities, the Confessing Church included members with a range of opinions and positions. Their reasons for rejecting the German Christians varied. Most raised concerns about converted Jews, but hardly any spoke up for unbaptized Jews. Not a few went so far as to be supportive of the Third Reich, leaving politics to the professionals as long as the church could go about its own spiritual business. Their main concern was that the state not meddle with the church, not that the state was setting in motion the slaughter of Jews. The Confessing Church publication, *Junge Kirche*, frequently vaunted its patriotic position in the face of war.

Despite this mixed record, the Third Reich became increasingly hostile toward the Confessing Church, and some of its members suffered because of their affiliation. This was especially true for those who were more clearly outspoken against Hitler such as Thielicke, Barth, who fled back to Switzerland, and Niemöller, who barely survived imprisonment in two concentration camps. Some lesser-known clergy also took risks and faced grim consequences, but overall, the Confessing Church was never the powerful voice on behalf of Jews that I had learned it to be. As one scholar of the German churches during the Third Reich put it:

> The Confessing Church concentrated too much on the confessing question . . . .While Christians discussed Romans 9-11 for five years, seeking clarity on whether and how Christians were 'allowed' to help Jews and non-Aryan Christians, the timetables for the deportation trains were being prepared in Nazi headquarters.

Our churches seem to love slow, drawn-out debates while lives hang in the balance.

Dietrich Bonhoeffer was an exception. He insisted on "The church's unconditional obligation to the victims of every social order, even those who do not belong to the Christian congregation." He was disillusioned at the lack of church outcry following *Kristallnacht* and told his students at the underground seminary he led, "Only those who cry out for the Jews can sing the Gregorian Chant." He spoke of "not only binding up the wounds of the victims under the wheel, but stopping the wheel itself," which led to his own participation in a plot to assassinate Hitler. Bonhoeffer was taken to Tegel Prision, then Buchenwald, and finally to Flossenbürg concentration camp where he was hanged on April 9, 1945.

***

If the German church, including the majority of Lutherans, had had their way, I would not be alive. The church, in both silence and speech, helped to advance the murder of millions. With this legacy, how can I be a Lutheran pastor? Why don't I flee to the side of my Jewish ancestors? I am a part of my Jewish ancestors, and I am a Christian with a slaughtered Jew at the center of my faith, a Jew I can no more disown than I can disown my own family. Jesus is quoted as saying, "Foxes have holes, and birds of the air have nests; but the Son of Man has nowhere to lay his head" (Luke 9:58 NRSV). Now, with him, I feel strangely dislodged.

CHAPTER FOUR

NEW YORK

When my plane lands back in New York, it's not just the time zone shift that requires adjustment. I need to reorient my thoughts away from a past that keeps tugging on me in order to focus on the tasks that await. I am grateful that my congregation is supportive of this endeavor and the time I've been taking to travel and write. Although I use vacation time to travel and write on my day off and in other spare moments, I still feel guilty about the tremendous interior attention this project absorbs. Once home, I want to make up for lost time, and so I often rush into my work each day instead of pausing first to pray as pastors should. Thankfully, I'm not left to deal with this failure on my own.

We have a prayer group that meets on Wednesday mornings, and Tanya arrived early while I was setting up. Tanya is raising her three grandchildren because their mother is in and out of drug treatment programs. They have special needs, and Tanya does her best to keep up with them despite her own physical challenges. On Sunday mornings, by 9:15, she has them up, dressed, fed and clamoring to light the candles for Wee Worship. They're usually the first ones here. She loves them wholeheartedly, and they know it. They are also wildly expressive of their affection, especially Serenity who is seven years old. Her hugs always pull me irresistibly into the present moment.

One week, our seminary student, Sara, had prepared a Sunday School lesson on Tabitha, a beloved leader in the early church. Tabitha was well-known for her good works, especially sewing clothing for widows. Sara told the story of how the widows mourned Tabitha's death and came to Peter holding up tunics she had woven for them. She told the children that Peter had raised Tabitha from her deathbed. Then Sara panicked. She remembered that there was a little boy in the class whose baby brother had recently died. Wouldn't Lucas wonder why God didn't make his little brother come back to life? Why God hadn't answered his prayers and those of his parents? Before Sara could figure out what to say, the usually shy and silent Lucas began to speak. He told the class that his little brother died and that Jesus raised his brother too and that his brother was with Jesus in heaven and that his brother was still with him. He showed the class a special woven bracelet that he and his parents now wore in memory of his brother in the same way that the widows must have shown Peter their woven tunics. The class, which includes children on medication for ADHD who get a break from their meds on weekends, sat perfectly still. Every eye and every ear was focused on the words of their Sunday school classmate who had walked in the valley of the shadow of death and was speaking about it.

Serenity spontaneously got up and gave her classmate a hug. Following her example, every child in the class got up and, one by one, hugged Lucas... and his father who was sitting to the side. After they sat back down, they wove paper placements for a Thanksgiving dinner that would be shared by hundreds the following Thursday—brightly colored paper woven in and out to grace the tables where the hungry gather to eat. Tanya brought her three grandchildren to that meal. Serenity was thrilled to notice the placemats, which she proudly pointed out.

Tanya tells me about this when she arrives for the prayer group and then, I see that she is crying. I've put out the batik tablecloth, Bibles, matches, and a candle, but didn't think of tissues. Tanya tells me that she needs surgery for gallstones and is worried about the children. Can she trust her daughter to get them to and from school? What if something happens to them and they are removed from her care? Tanya's stress is raising her blood pressure—which makes her more anxious. Then she tells me her secret. Tanya had another daughter born with full-blown AIDS in the 1980s. Experimental AZT gave her two years instead of the predicted six months, but she died in December and the anniversary is coming up.

Tanya never speaks about this daughter because to speak of the child is to speak of her own diagnosis. She's afraid that people will judge her and "treat her funny." She's afraid that she will not be allowed to adopt her grandchildren. She tells me the baby's name was Danielle. She didn't realize she was positive at the time and lives with guilt for passing on the virus that took her little girl's life. She's afraid that others will condemn her for her ignorance and for the living daughter's problems, but she's already condemned herself.

I remember the early 80s and the many funerals I did for young mothers who died of AIDS in the South Bronx. My present congregation has a garden behind the church with roses and ferns and a fig tree where I'm told that the ashes of some early AIDS victims are buried. Funeral homes did not want to touch their bodies and some cemeteries didn't want their remains. That was thirty years ago, but the stigma persists. When a young man in our shelter tested positive, his first reaction was that he wanted to kill himself. He feared being sick, but he also dreaded being a pariah among his peers.

Tanya has several photos of Danielle that she hides well, but she's afraid that the children will find them. She waits to be sure they are all asleep before she takes the pictures out and worries that one of the children might awaken and catch her gazing at Danielle. She rarely does this though, because she says that her crying might not be good for her health. I tend to think that uncried tears turn into something worse than gallstones. Tanya has taught Serenity the grace of comforting others, but she herself has not been comforted.

* * *

Now Tanya is sobbing and wiping her nose on her sleeve. I run to get the tissues and let her sob, hoping for more time before the others arrive for prayer. As she cries, I think of my father. I see him beside her, bearing his own unspoken secret, guilt, and loss. My father cried more readily than my mother, but I rarely saw his tears spill beyond the rim of his eyelids. He traveled for work quite a bit, and I wonder if he saved his sobs for the privacy of the hotel rooms in cities my mother and I marked with sticky stars on a map in my bedroom. Or perhaps, he just never allowed himself the release. Like Tanya, like everyone who bears a secret burden, he never received any direct comfort for the sorrow he could not name. No one around him could guess the depth of his loss and what it meant for him. My father and Tanya led such very different lives, and yet I see them as twins in their hidden grief and perhaps in the lingering fear of stigma. When my father was the age of the young man in our shelter, to be a Jew was to be genetically contaminated. Like HIV in the early 80s, it became a death sentence.

* * *

Tanya's tears are subsiding and she accepts a hug. With a shaky smile, she agrees that when our little group assembles we will pray for her surgery, her grandchildren, their mother, and even the up-coming anniversary. This is part of my work—to hear the secret stories of hurt and anger, addiction and abuse, health problems not ready for public notice, infidelities, shame, and guilt. I listen. I pray. I weep. I absolve. Sometimes I hear things that make me want to scream or strangle someone who is not in the room, but that is my own secret. What I could never do for my father, I do for others. Germany is across the ocean. My research in Lübeck and my work in New York have felt like competing pulls on my attention, but today the differences dissolve.

CHAPTER FIVE

BERLIN

HITLER YOUTH

In the summer of 2010, a year after my trip to Wittmund and Lübeck with Hans, I returned to Europe. My main purpose was to visit Theresienstadt, but I wanted to follow up on some other leads including my family's final days in Berlin. Seven decades earlier, my father's sister, Susy, made her way to Berlin in advance of my grandparents, shortly after Hitler became chancellor in 1933. She moved from Hamburg with her three children, Klaus, Ursula and Peter.

I knew my Aunt Susy, who visited our home a number of times during my childhood and college years. She also took care of me in Switzerland when my parents went to Paris for second honeymoon and left me in Gstaad where Oma lived in a beautiful chalet for the elderly. Aunt Susy and I visited Oma daily and I remember coloring many pictures for her. One day Oma presented me with a sewing card, needle, and some yarn. It was designed to make the outline of a cat beside a flower. Oma told me that her neighbor in the chalet would be happy to have such a picture because she was blind and could feel it with her fingers. I worked the yarn through the holes while Oma and Susy chatted in German.

Throughout the time I knew her, Susy's home base was in Brazil with Klaus' family, and for the last few years of her life, in Australia with her daughter Ursula. When travel plans brought her through New York, she'd come to see us in New Jersey. She spoke English perfectly, but there was never any talk of Judaism or the Shoah. It would not have occurred to me to ask her about it. My cousins Ursula and Peter have both died, so I've had to rely on Klaus to fill me in. I've also talked via Skype with Ursula's daughter Barbara, who is my age and remains living in Australia.

During World War I, Susy married an army officer who was Roman Catholic, but she never practiced his faith. They divorced before her move to Berlin with their three children. At the time, Klaus was twelve years old, Ursula was ten and Peter was eight. On the day before Klaus was to begin at his new school, Susy informed him that he was descended from Jews on her side of the family. As had happened with my father, he was told because his parents didn't want him to grow up to become a Nazi. Klaus only said to me that he was "astonished" and that he didn't know anything about Jews or attitudes against Jews, but that didn't last.

Soon after Klaus entered school in Berlin, his teacher announced that all Jewish children should come and stand in front of the class. Klaus remained in his seat. Then she ordered all half-Jews to come forward, and Klaus complied. It was a lesson in racial hygiene to familiarize students with "perfect specimens of a despised race." Klaus blames himself for the misery that followed, saying that he should have stayed in his seat. From then on, he said that he was persecuted and felt defenseless and that he didn't want to go to school any more. He was taunted and harassed and said, "The propaganda against Jews was so intensive everywhere, and everyone was influenced not to like Jews or any descendants of Jews." He hated to salute and say "Heil Hitler" whenever the teacher entered and in every store, but it was the law. He began to get stomachaches every morning before school and begged his mother not to make him go.

This seems far from the multiracial mix in my own city's public schools until I remember a girl named Tamia crying in the bathroom to the point of throwing up at church while the others were doing an art project. A group of her classmates had taken to calling her an ugly African monkey, and the thought of returning to school on Monday was making her sick. While it was not a daily racial hygiene lesson from the teacher, those in authority did nothing to protect Tamia. Living in a neighborhood where racial profiling is business as usual and seeing news clips of young, unarmed African Americans killed by those in authority added to her sense of vulnerability and worthlessness.

Klaus' stomachaches led Susy to move him to another school where he was able to hide his Jewish roots. His new teacher did not talk much about Jews, and he felt safer. Like Renate, he began to live a closeted identity. During this period, Peter went to school without problems. Sadly, Barbara told me that her mother, Ursula, was kept home because it was safer for her to stay away from official attention in school. I remember Ursula as a very warm, kind, and intelligent woman. Her husband was a nuclear physicist. I never realized that Ursula's own education had been aborted.

When he turned fourteen, Klaus had to join the Hitler Youth, which became mandatory for all Aryan boys of his age. He remembers it as a fun time, like being a Boy Scout, and he went on weekend excursions with biking, hiking, and camping. He made no mention of the propaganda. Klaus enjoyed being accepted but knew that his belonging was predicated on a lie that could be exposed at any moment. It must have been a terrible psychological strain for a young teen, one endured by many other assimilated young people whose parents converted or who had been born of interfaith marriages. Like my father, Klaus suppressed his inner turmoil. They didn't fit in as Jews or as Aryans. When I met with Dr. Ismar Schorsch, chancellor-emeritus of the Jewish Theological Seminary in Manhattan, he told me that he thought the period was especially hard for those who were alienated from their Jewish roots and could therefore not experience solidarity with the Jewish community and yet were no longer considered part of German society either.

In 1936 Klaus had not yet been found out. He was the only one in his Hitler Youth group who played the trumpet, and he was chosen to play at the 1936 Olympics in Berlin, which my father also attended. The Olympic Games brought a brief respite from outward shows of anti-Semitism, especially in Berlin. To appease the international community, propaganda posters were taken down, and Nazi publications were temporarily suspended and removed from newsstands. I have my father's box of photographs showing the streets of Berlin decorated with Nazi and Olympic flags as well as the opening ceremony and many events. He took a number of photographs composed to feature a giant hand outstretched in the Nazi salute over the crowds of spectators. He also captured the release of thirty thousand pigeons, a symbol of peace dwarfed by the monstrous hand. At one point, Klaus climbed a tree to take a picture of Hitler and was forced down by the police and given a warning. It was now a crime to be physically higher than the Führer.

A GREEN SHADE

1936 was also the year my grandparents moved to Berlin with their youngest daughter, my Aunt Lore, while my father remained in

Lübeck at the iron works. The Grunewald area they chose remains one of Berlin's poshest. My friend Carsten, who lives in Berlin, looked up the address prior to my visit and took me to find the house. We passed a number of ambassadors' residences on our way. Grunewald, literally "green forest," is a neighborhood of large, stately homes with numerous old trees taller than the houses. There is ample space for gracious lawns, shrubbery, and gardens. I visited in the summer and felt enveloped by a calming aura of green sunlight filtering through green leaves of every shade. Carsten and I walked from the train station to the house, passing over a small bridge called the *Hansensprung* or Rabbit Jump Bridge. The bridge was built across two lakes bordered by more trees. We were looking for the Koenigsalle, a well-known street in the area.

In the 1920s and 30s, there were frequent evening soirees with readings and concerts in the neighborhood including at the home of the Bonhoeffer family who lived in Grunewald for a time. About a third of these entertainments were held and frequented by Jews. Guests included Franz and Robert Mendelssohn, bankers descended from the Jewish philosopher Moses Mendelssohn, Max Reinhardt, the theater director, Samuel Fischer, who founded one of Germany's major publishing houses, and Walther Rathenau, who became the foreign minister of the Weimar Republic. He also wrote a controversial book called *Hear O Israel* in 1897 in which he proposes the full assimilation of German Jews, a vision embraced wholeheartedly by my grandfather.

Rathenau was a contemporary of Moritz, born just a year later. They knew each other through industrial and political connections. Rathenau was active in the DDP, German Democratic Party, supported by many Jews, the party that my grandfather represented when he was elected to Lübeck's senate in 1919. In 1922 Rathenau was shot and killed by some ultra-nationalists. A stone marking the spot of his assassination is on the Koenigsallee, not far from my grandparents' new home. His murder, however, was not the norm for this cultured area that had long welcomed well-connected Jews.

We reached their residence at Koenigsallee 28. In 1930 the house was divided into luxury apartments, and my grandparents rented one of them. At the time in Berlin, many Jews were finding their leases cancelled followed by their eviction. There was a steady increase in economic boycotts against Jews, who were also being barred from clubs and many restaurants. It was not uncommon to see swimming pools with signs warning off "Jews and dogs." The Nuremberg Laws had gone into effect the previous year, and only those with "German blood" could be considered as full citizens with rights.

Despite this growing hostility towards Jews, there were no uniformed Nazis patrolling the very civilized streets of Grunewald when my grandparents settled into their green oasis. There was nothing to stop them from going out for walks in the lush parks, over the Rabbit Jump Bridge, under a protective canopy of trees. For my grandparents in 1936, Grunewald brought Andrew Marvell's poem to life: "Annihilating all that's made / To a green thought in a green shade." How bad could things really be?

AN ALIEN IN MESHECH

Woe is me, that I am an alien in Meshech,
That I must live among the tents of Kedar.
Too long have I had my dwelling
Among those who hate peace.

—Psalm 120:5-6 NRSV

Although my grandfather refused to believe that his own life and that of my grandmother were in any real danger, he took no chances with his children and began to organize their escape. Susy and her husband had remarried but now he left her again, fearing what might happen if he remained married to a Jew. Susy didn't want to leave Germany, worried that in the process she might be separated from her children, so my grandfather arranged for her to travel to England, where she would marry a Mr. Stanley who was willing to help her obtain an English passport. Barbara in Australia told me that in exchange for the marriage, Susy gave Mr. Stanley a typewriter and my grandfather gave him whatever he required financially. Susy returned to Berlin with her life-saving passport and never saw Mr. Stanley again. She also moved with her children to a house in Dahlem, a village that had become part of Berlin, yet retained its suburban feel.

Lore was sent to England to stay for the duration. What happened to Lore during the war years in London is a mystery. There is no one to ask but Klaus and Renate, who only told me that Lore had "a very, very hard life." At some point, she learned that her parents had been taken by the Nazis but had no idea where they were or what was happening to them. She was not only the youngest child, but the neediest, more pampered and emotionally fragile than Susy or my father. Eventually, she learned that her father did not survive and whatever else her mother would tell her.

We know that in 1950, Lore was permitted to become a naturalized English citizen. Two months later, she would marry Victor Wollner, a Czechoslovakian Jew who had experienced his own journey of serial dislocation. In the thirties, he worked in a steel mill in Vienna (and was perhaps known to Moritz?). In 1938 he returned to Prague. In 1939 he was registered under the Czech quota for Jewish refugees and then traveled to Paris, to Spain and finally to the United States by way of South America. He arrived in New York on the S.S. *Brazil* in 1941 and became a naturalized citizen in 1947. I discovered this in another envelope of papers saved by Lore.

After the war, Victor worked for the U.S. government in Germany and Italy for several years. I have no idea how he and Lore met or knew each other, but they were married by a clerk in Wiesbaden, Germany, in the U.S. zone. Victor is noted as being "*Israelitisch*" and Lore as "*Protestantisch.*" A month later, Victor petitioned the United States for a visa so that Lore could emigrate. In order to do this, their marriage certificate was translated into English and certified by the U.S. Consul in Naples, Italy.

So, a Czechoslovakian Jew marries a German Jew, now English and Protestant, in Germany, under U.S. control, and they go to Italy to get the documents needed to emigrate to the United States. Like many survivors, they found refuge under a crazy quilt of shifting borders. Lore arrived at LaGuardia Airfield on a TWA flight before the end of 1950. She settled in New York and became a U.S. citizen, but she never really regained her footing.

Lore worked as a clerk/typist for Helena Rubinstein, the MacMillan Company, and for long years, in the library of The American Institute of Accountants. She and Victor, who was fourteen years her senior, never had any children. He died six years after they were married. My parents and I were then Lore's only family in the United States.

* * *

Lore rented an apartment in Queens. Our home in New Jersey was only an hour away, and we saw her frequently. I remembered steeling myself for the rush of anxiety she unleashed the moment she stepped into our house. Tante Lore was a hive of nerves. She couldn't sit still, and she talked nonstop in English with frequent eruptions in German, *"Nicht? Nicht?"* Her nervousness spread through our house like a contagion. Our two dachshunds, calm as far as dachshunds go, ran in crazed circles barking whenever she crossed our threshold.

One of the first things Aunt Lore would do was go to my room and look through my closet checking to see what, if anything, had changed. She would also go through my drawers and look at the carefully arranged items on my dresser. Sometimes I would find her on the floor looking under my bed. We all just accepted these strange, invasive activities.

One day, however, when I was around twelve, she came into the bathroom when I was in the shower. I felt that she was trying to watch me. Our shower had frosted glass, but I felt exposed and yelled at her to leave. After that, I locked the door.

Aunt Lore also had an odd behavior around food. Chocolate had a sacramental quality that I discovered when I ate a piece of Swiss chocolate she had put in our refrigerator and she became unreasonably agitated. I thought it was to be shared, which was true, but it was to be on her terms, when she parceled it out ceremoniously. For me, as a teenager, it seemed like a lot of hullabaloo over a small square of chocolate.

My father had no patience for his sister's eccentricities, while my mother tried to smooth things over. Lore's nervousness, her many neurotic ticks, her hoarding, checking, and other obsessive-compulsive habits all made my father very uncomfortable. He wanted her to act normally. Her behavior must have bought up things he wanted to avoid. She was a living, breathing reminder of so much that had not been normal. Renate told me that she believes my father had sworn Lore to secrecy about the past he wanted hidden, and this likely increased her anxiety when she was with us. It surely raised his own tension level with her, too. Her obvious suffering may also have piqued his guilt. No wonder her visits were exhausting. I loved Aunt Lore but was always relieved when she left.

In the last decade of her life, Lore had a tumor that required brain surgery, a further trauma that intensified her neurotic behavior. Eventually, she needed assisted living, which my mother arranged. We visited her every week, and after my father died, my mother continued to care for her sister-in-law. It became more difficult as Lore's obsessive-compulsive behavior escalated. She demanded that my mother bring cucumber face cream at every visit, even though there were multiple unopened jars in her closet. She was equally anxious about the exacting placement of furniture, pillows and picture frames that the cleaning staff would sometimes move.

My mother and I would talk, trying to guess what made Aunt Lore the way she was. My mother thought that when Lore was a child, she had been made to sing at my grandparents' big dinner parties to entertain the guests. She had her beautiful voice, but she was very shy. My mother conjectured that this singing for company had launched a lifetime of nervousness. I began to think that she may have been sexually abused as a child or young adult, perhaps in England during the war. This was all fantastical guesswork.

Now I can see my aunt through a different lens. She was a hidden victim of the Shoah. She survived, but she lived with post-traumatic stress that was never recognized or treated. We didn't have any appropriate labels to use. She was "nutty Aunt Lore" and "nosy Aunt Lore." No one had heard of OCD or PTSD, and I'm not sure if the labels would have changed anything. Perhaps, we would have tried to get her therapy or medication and maybe it would have helped. As it was, she had no community to turn to for understanding. If she had been a Jew by faith, she might have found support and under-standing for her burden. Instead, she went to church regularly and kept silent.

My father mellowed toward his sister over time, and my mother cared for Lore with infinite patience. Many people suffered more and coped better than Lore, including my grandmother, but Lore did not have that strength. She survived. She had some good friends. She loved us. She never missed a day of work, but something in her would never be right again.

Now I have a different insight into the sorrowful source of this family drama. I remember the last time I saw Aunt Lore alive. I was home from seminary and drove to the nursing home to see her. The staff told me that she had regressed to speaking only in the German of her childhood that none of them could understand. They said that she kept repeating one word in particular which they hoped I could translate. I went into her room. I'm not sure how aware she was of my presence, my voice, or my touch. I held her hand and listened. The little German I knew was enough to understand the word she kept repeating like a mournful mantra until she could speak no more: *allein, allein, allein*—alone.

I feel fresh grief for my aunt. I wish I could go back in time to approach her differently. Instead, I walked from our home to an ad-dress that I found in her papers, the first apartment she lived in when she came to New York before settling in Queens. It was a mere eight blocks from my church and the parsonage where I live, and I had passed it many times.

The front of the building had a decorative concrete garland of flower medallions around the glass doors and iron gates. It was unlocked, and I went inside. A second set of doors beyond the entryway was locked. The space between the two sets of doors became my memorial chapel. I had planned to read, Psalm 121: "The Lord will protect you on your journeys—whether going or coming—from now until forever from now." Then my eye fell on Psalm 120 which seemed even more apt, a cry of distress from the displaced and violated. Both psalms are songs of ascent, thought to have been sung by pilgrims making their way up through rough terrain to Jerusalem. Lore herself had ceased to sing as she wandered through the brutal geography that rose up before her.

No one else was around, so I prayed the words of the psalm aloud. I longed to trace the lines on the lintel. I wished them to fly back in time to embrace the lost young woman I knew as my aunt. I had thought about bringing flowers or a candle, but the residents would wonder who in the building had died. I can only hope that her ascent is complete and she is at peace. I filled the space with psalms and left their syllables floating like petals through the air.

THE ARK

. . . the earth had become corrupt and was filled with violence.

—Genesis 6:11

My father's sisters, Susy and Lore, each began her wartime odyssey by crossing the North Sea to England. My father would go farther, across the ocean, into the arms of the Statue of Liberty, who offered an unequivocal welcome, or so I assumed.

As a child and young woman, I was not much of a history student, but my zeal to learn about my father's family led to obsessive reading of the very history books I once ignored. Two books in particular, both by David Wyman, helped me understand more about my father's move to the United States. The first, *Paper Walls,* covers the refugee crisis from 1938 when my father emigrated up to 1941, when the doors shut. The second, *The Abandonment of the Jews,* continues the tragic story through to the end of the war in 1945.

As Nazi terror increased in the late 1930s, so did the economic recession under Roosevelt. Refugees were seen as competitors for scant jobs and resources, and there was a growing suspicion of Jewish immigrants as outsiders who posed a cultural and racial threat. In 1939, Nazi sympathizers held a large rally in Madison Square Garden. In that same year, the New York Chamber of Commerce published a paper called "Conquest by Immigration" that sounds like it was prepared by a Tea Party candidate. In addition to taking jobs from "real" Americans, it points out that among immigrants, there are a large number of criminals and people seeking to go on the "relief rolls."

Anti-Semitism was at an all-time high and growing when my father arrived here in 1938. When it came to fear-mongering, religious figures took the lead. Father Charles Coughlin from Michigan had a weekly tabloid and radio broadcast that reached fifteen million listeners. He justified the attacks of *Kristallnacht* as a reasonable defense against Communism. His broadcasts rode a wave of hate. The most anti-Semitic part of the country was the urban northeast, where my father would land to start his new life. Boston and New York City were the worst. By 1941, almost every synagogue in Manhattan's Washington Heights had been desecrated. In Boston, Jewish cemetery desecrations were commonplace. In both cities, Jewish children were regularly attacked by teenage gangs whose members were all found to have been influenced by anti-Semitic propaganda they were exposed to at home or in school.

When Germany overtook Austria in March of 1938, the international community was shaken into attention. President Roosevelt responded immediately by calling a conference of thirty-two nations to develop a joint plan to better deal with the growing crisis of refugees from Nazi territories. During the meeting near Lake Geneva, it was soon clear that each country was looking for the others to take responsibility. A *Newsweek* reporter summed it up: "Chairman Myron C. Taylor, former United States Steel head, opened proceedings: 'The time has come when governments . . . must act and act promptly.' Most governments represented acted promptly by slamming their doors against Jewish refugees."

The majority of U.S. citizens continued to give lip service to the condemnation of what little the media told them about Nazi persecution, but in 1938 polls showed that over eighty percent of the population opposed increasing quotas for refugees. President Roosevelt did not believe he could challenge this resistance, and he didn't. Once the war began in 1939, only 21,000 Jewish refugees were permitted to enter, just ten percent of the number allowed by immigrant quotas at the time.

By 1940 there was an additional obstacle for refugees. Nazis were purportedly disguising themselves as Jewish refugees in order to spy from within the United States. The *Readers Digest* published three articles that lent legitimacy to this new fear. Now the refugees were suspect as an ever more sinister presence:

Attorney General Robert Jackson was "plainly worried about the disposition, in various parts of the country, of local authorities, and even irresponsible groups, to go out on a 'spy hunt."' Hysteria is sweeping the country against aliens . . . People are breaking into other people's houses and confronting them with a flag demanding that they salute it. Down in Georgia, Governor Rivers has promptly declared war on all aliens . . . it might be necessary for the Government actually to indict some prominent local or state officials in order to make it known to the country that we were not being ruled by disorderly mobs.

It's impossible for me to read this and not think of citizen militias arming themselves against "aliens" today. Or of racial profiling and neighborhood "watchmen" like George Zimmerman prowling their communities to target African American men and boys. By 1941 the Statue of Liberty was no longer welcoming Jews yearning to breathe free and by late spring of that year there was no longer any legal exit from Nazi occupied lands. There were advocates for the Jews during this period, mostly from Jewish organizations, but also some Christians. These voices and groups helped many of those who made it here, but they were unable to leverage any major policy shift when it was needed most.

In the end, the United States received about 250,000 refugees, more than any other nation. We could have absorbed many more, but even those who recoiled at overt acts of anti-Semitism, supported a closed-door policy that consigned hundreds of thousands to their deaths. The many soldiers who gave their lives to a war that led to the defeat of Hitler and the liberation of death camps deserve their honored place in history as I learned it. The shameful handcuffing of liberty in a time of dire need must also be taught and told.

* * *

When my father boarded the ship that would carry him to safety in 1938, it was not his first voyage to these shores. In 1930, my grandfather sent him on an educational tour to the United States and to Asia. For eight months my father traveled the world as a curious, dedicated scientist and as a young man having a great adventure, not a refugee fleeing for his life. The point of the trip was to expand his knowledge of global trends beyond Europe that would be relevant to his future work at the helm of his father's business, but it turned out to prepare him for a future in the United States. I now realize the likely reason my father was immediately hired by the Pyrites Company when he emigrated: he had already visited the firm on his trip and met many of the key players, whose names he typed in his journal. It was almost eight years before he would seek employment there, but it seems obvious that those connections made a difference. He probably wrote to them before he embarked.

Following this journey, my father returned home to work as the superintendent of the copper works branch of the blast furnace. At that point, everything was unfolding perfectly. It was wonderful that my father's own interest and ability matched his father's dreams for him. I understood that the war had interrupted their happy plans, but not the heinous nature of the events to follow. In less than two years after the trip, my grandfather was writing his "Here I Stand" letter to Herr Fabry, who was conspiring to rob both father and son of the future toward which they had both so passionately labored.

As I wrote earlier, my father was permitted to remain at his post with the copper works until he left Germany, most certainly because no one could be found who was better suited for the task, and the Nazis needed the plant to function smoothly.

By 1938 the status of Jews in Germany was quickly deteriorating. My grandfather, perhaps pushed by my grandmother, arranged with my father for him to leave. The United States would only give visas to those who had someone willing to provide a financial guarantee that they would not become "a charge of the state." My father's old college friend, Gus Luttringhaus, prepared the required documents, and my father got his exit visa on February 28, 1938, in Hamburg. On May 27 he boarded the S.S. *Europa* in Bremen and arrived in New York harbor on the 2nd of June.

There was a brief window in the beginning of 1938 where Jewish emigrants could take up to 50,000 Reich Marks out of the country. My father left four days before the policy ended.

In addition, he was able to bring many trunks, bearing boxes of his numerous photographs, the oil painting over our piano, Kachina dolls and a Chinese rug from his earlier travels, family silver (we never ate fish without the silver fish forks, each engraved with an ornate N), and books—volumes about Lübeck, the iron works, and leather bound volumes of Goethe and Schiller, the heart and soul of cultured Germany. All of this he carried across the waters, along with his confirmation certificate and his Lutheran faith. He would never regain the lifestyle he had once known, and he often described the early years of starting from scratch, but he did not arrive as a pauper.

I wonder what went through his mind during the days of his ocean crossing, so different from the first voyage when the ship manifest listed him only as German, without mention of "Hebrew." Fortunate as he was to be on the S.S. *Europa*, I doubt that he felt particularly lucky. Besides his trunks, he bore a weight of loss and, likely, guilt over leaving his aging parents, despite their insistence that he go. To guilt was added worry, for them, and for the sisters, nephews, and niece he left behind. I also imagine that he felt angry and help-less to change anything, other than his own destiny.

As his saving ark neared the shores of a new land, my father de-cided to fling himself into a wholly new beginning. I'm sure that the rising tide of anti-Semitism in the late thirties in the United States contributed to his choices. He had never embraced his Jewish iden-tity before, and it wasn't timely to admit to that part of his history now. He landed, holding on to a vanishing past of Goethe and silver fish forks, and about to begin his own disappearing act.

Dark Rooms

Susy and her children remained in Berlin, where Klaus finished high school and was ready for the university but first, all students were required to complete at least six months of *Reichsarbeitsdienst,* or Reich Labor Service. To Klaus' relief and surprise, his *Mischling* status continued to remain undiscovered. His service unit was dis-patched to Norway and Klaus asked the company leader if he could take along his photographic equipment. Instead of laboring with his comrades, Klaus was allowed to pass the time taking pictures to pro-vide a photographic record while others lugged heavy sacks of saw-dust and barrels of water out onto a glacier to fill cracks and prepare the ice to serve as an air field. For their accommodations, the Nazis took over a resort where Klaus said the staff continued preparing their meals and cleaning their rooms and even their boots.

This rather idyllic time in Norway could not last. Klaus returned to Berlin to work in a grenade-making factory. The operation moved to southern Germany, not far from the Dachau concentration camp. He found a room to rent in a farmhouse and was allowed to shower at his job. When describing this to me decades later, Klaus expressed no qualms about making grenades and repeatedly described himself to me as "very lucky." It seemed that he had managed to disassociate himself from what he was actually doing. He believed that he was fortunate to have found this path to survival.

At some point in 1942, Klaus' luck ran out. His secret was uncovered, and he was sent to a labor camp for half-Jews and non-Jews who had committed the crime of marrying Jews. The camp was not far from Dresden. One day, they asked who could drive a truck, and Klaus raised his hand, although he'd only ever driven a car. Lucky once again, he got the job of transporting others to various work areas around the camp, work that was much easier than the heavy labor that awaited his passengers. Their job was to clean and rebuild a factory. When the work was completed, everyone at the labor camp was called to line up and prepare to leave. They were forced to march in single file into the forest with guns pointed at them on both sides. It was a very dark night, with heavy clouds obscuring the moon. Klaus slowed his step and in a second, when no eye was on him, he slipped behind a tree. Klaus was certain that they would hear his bellowing heart, but the death march continued without him. His luck held. He walked until he reached some train tracks and was able to sneak onto the train and hide in the bathroom. Klaus made his way to Berlin without being caught.

Back home in Berlin, Klaus hid for the rest of the war, never once leaving the house, and retreating to the attic whenever there was a knock at the door.

GLORY, LAUD AND HONOR

Why didn't my grandparents leave? Why didn't they leave when my father left, or even somewhat later, before it was impossible?

Between 1933 and 1939, fifty-seven percent of Germany's Jews emigrated. It was increasingly difficult to get out, but my grandparents still had plenty of money, and if anyone could have managed, they could have. They were elderly, but my grandmother would live for another quarter century. Who knows how long my grandfather could have lived? He would have been eighty-eight when I was born. I might have seen him face to face and sat in his lap and played with his glasses. They would have avoided so much suffering.

My grandparents' strength was also their downfall. They were optimists. Despite everything, they refused to believe that Hitler would remain unchecked. My grandfather could not comprehend that the country he fought for, worked for and loved, would murder him. It was simply inconceivable, and he had the talismans to prove it. I have in my possession an honorary silver dish inscribed for his fiftieth birthday:

Honor to whom honor is due
As merits to a crown
Herr General Direktor, Dr. Neumark
On his 50th day.

Embedded in the center of the dish is a silver 1748 Lübeck 32 schilling, one side showing the city seal. In spite of his ouster from the iron works and the attendant losses, Moritz kept this ornate dish, a sign of the way things had been, the way things were supposed to be but also, I think, a sign of hope for the future. Hitler was a temporary aberration. My grandfather's reflection in the shining silver surface of the dish told a different story. At some point, however, he did hand the dish over to Susy.

My Opa's stubborn hope was abetted by an article in his hometown paper. It was 1941. Germany's occupying army was advancing through Europe. Jews were not allowed to own radios and had to turn them in along with typewriters and appliances at local police stations. Jews could not buy new clothes, had to obey a curfew, could not drive, go to the movies, or use public phone booths. Many were forced from their homes as part of the "De-Judification of Living Space." Jews were stripped of their German citizenship. They were no longer allowed to take German names, and if they had them already, like my grandparents, they had to take the additional name of Israel or Sarah. My grandparents became Ida Sarah Neumark and Moritz Israel Neumark. They could not sign any document without this enforced identity. Like all Jews at that time, they were required to wear a yellow star inscribed with the word "*Jude.*"

In the midst of this mounting humiliation and repression, an article appeared in the Wittmund newspaper, dated Pentecost of 1941. On the occasion of his seventy-fifth birthday, my grandfather was feted as a hometown boy who made good, the son of a local merchant. It was a lengthy feature that chronicled Moritz's entire educational and work history. Wittmund was proud to congratulate him on this special occasion. No mention was made of the fact that he had been stripped of his job and all public posts. No mention was made of the fact that he was a Neumark Jew. Is it possible that an editor in Wittmund failed to know this? I can only imagine that this peculiar birthday homage burnished my grandfather's illusory sense of hope. Pentecost came in the late spring. By that fall, the deportations of Berlin's Jews would begin.

Meanwhile, the methodical stripping away of my grandparents' lives continued. They could no longer enjoy walks in the woodland paths near their home because public parks were off-limits to Jews. They were not allowed to buy newspapers or listen to the radios that would soon be confiscated. Private phones were disconnected, and public phones were off limits. The Jews of Berlin faced local laws that went beyond the repressive laws of the Third Reich. Entire sections of the city were closed to Jews, along with growing number of businesses, restaurants, and shops. Buildings where Jews where known to live were marked to make the eventual process of deportation all the easier.

My grandparents had to report every month at a designated police station. Klaus told me that the police were kind to them for a time and even went so far as to advise them on how best to stay out of trouble. Moritz gave money to the Nazi collection of winter relief help for the poor. When Jews were required to turn in appliances, typewriters, electronics, and jewels, my grandparents complied. Klaus became clearly upset in recalling the camera that was handed over to the Nazis instead of to him. He described Moritz as "so beaten in every way," but he also mentioned our grandfather's refusal to wear the star on the outside of his clothing, a tiny rebellion for which he might have been instantly killed. By that point, Moritz didn't go out much, and when he did, he wore the star under his coat and was never caught. Klaus said that our grandfather remained convinced that the Nazis wouldn't touch him because he had been so useful to Germany.

* * *

Hitler gave the order to rid Berlin of all Jews, and the systematic train transports began on October 18, 1941. It was Yom Kippur, the holiest of Jewish holidays. Ninety thousand Jews from Berlin had already emigrated, but over fifty-five thousand remained. Many of the trains left from Track 17 of the Grunewald railway station, a short walk from my grandparents' home, as did that first one on Yom Kippur, taking 1251 Jews to the Lodz Ghetto in Poland.

I walked to the station with my friend Carsten after we visited the site of my grandparents' Berlin home. The residents of Grunewald used the same railway and could not have been ignorant of the crowds of Jews across the track. Every month, from October of 1941 through March of 1945, hundreds of Berliners, in full, public view, were led to the trains and, ultimately, cattle cars that would carry them to their deaths. Of course, by that time, Jews were no longer viewed as "Berliners."

The train industry knew what they were doing and benefited from the procedures, netting two Deutsche Marks per passenger and an additional four pfennigs per kilometer for each adult transported, and half that for children. There was little blood spilled as the trains pulled in and left with their cargo, but Track 17 is a grisly place, a tree-lined gateway to hell.

In the 1950s, a group of elderly women from a church near the Grunewald Station put up a small memorial that fell apart when they grew too old to care for it. They at least were willing to acknowledge the crime scene. It was not until 1991 that the German government commissioned a memorial. Today, if you go to the still-used station, you must pass a concrete wall pocked by the hollow silhouettes of deportees. When you walk by their shadowy imprints down a tunnel toward Track 17 and up the stairs, you come to an additional memorial installed by the German Railways, one that does not allow you to stand and observe. You must walk into it, through it, and on it, beside the tracks themselves, now overgrown with grasses and shrubs. You walk on an iron grid laid beside the tracks with iron plates, one for each deportation train that left Berlin, each plate engraved with the date, destination, and number of deportees. The numbers add up with every step you take, week by week, month by month, train after train after train, carrying 50,000 Jews out of Berlin, carrying my grandparents: **28.1.1943 / 100 Juden / Theresienstadt.**

* * *

I read that seven thousand Jews in Berlin committed suicide when they got news of their impending deportation. Many more did what my grandparents did; they packed for the journey, carefully selecting, folding, stuffing as much as they could into the luggage they were allowed to carry with them. If possible, they contacted loved ones. Klaus remembers the night my grandparents phoned to say that the Gestapo would come for them in the morning. How did they manage to call when their phone had been disconnected? Somehow they did, and nearly seventy years later, Klaus becomes silent with the memory, newly helpless in the chill that clamped down upon them after the call, their uneaten supper grown cold. When his voice returned, Klaus told me that by then, everybody had heard about concentration camps but nobody really knew what was happening there: "We tried to find out but we didn't know, except we knew that it was bad."

The following morning, there was a knock on the door and a bus waiting to take Moritz and Ida away. I had believed that they went directly to Track 17, but the memorial was a bit misleading. It marks every transport that left Berlin, including those from other stations. By January of 1943, the trains were departing from two other sites. My grandparents were first taken to *Grosse Hamburger Strasse* 26, a

Jewish home for the elderly that had been converted into an assembly camp. They were held there for two or three days, enough time to make certain that all of their documents were in order and to coordinate lists of passengers and train schedules.

Prior to their arrest, they had been required to fill out a sixteen-page declaration of assets, part of a gross, legal fiction. All assets had to remain for the benefit of the German Reich, which meant that since my grandparents were going to be "traveling out of the country," most of what they owned had to be left behind. To ensure full compliance, they were strip-searched while their luggage was being sifted through for valuables. Jewish assets confiscated by the Nazis paid for thirty percent of the cost of World War II.

At the assembly camp, some were given contracts to complete, as if they were going to an old-age home or assisted-living facility, as they were told. One survivor recalls hearing shocked German Jews at Theresienstadt telling how they had paid for a safe haven in a spa-like town abroad that assured pleasant twilight years. Some Berliners had requested and paid for rooms with a lakeside view. I wondered if my grandparents fell for this sadistic ruse. They belonged under a "privileged" category that included Jews with war medals and some elderly. Most of them were going to be sent to Theresienstadt, although some went directly to their deaths at Auschwitz. At the time of their deportation, those were the only two destinations for the Jews of Berlin.

Did they really believe they were heading for a nice old-age home? After some research, I wrote to an office with government archives in Berlin to inquire if any records had survived of my grandparents entering into such a contract. It seemed a long-shot, but a few months later, a manila envelope arrived in the mail with a photocopy of the document—*Heimeinkaufvertrag* (Home Purchase Contract). I took it to church and asked several of our German members to translate it for me. They found it as mind-blowing as I did. My grandparents had indeed signed a contract, paying $199,750 DM, that would entitle them to good accommodations and meals at the senior living center to which they would be taken. Since the Reich would be paying for all who needed accommodations, part of my grandparents' fee would help those who were less fortunate. The contract was signed by Moritz Israel Neumark and Ida Sara Neumark on January 22, 1943. It's unclear if they signed this in the days just before their arrest or at the assembly camp. If it was at the camp, they would have been there for at least a week, which seems unusually long; therefore, it is more likely that they were called in to make these arrangements before their arrest. The fact that they signed the contract does not mean that they believed its promises, but it feels likely to me that they, along with many others, continued to hope for the best because anything else was still unthinkable.

While my grandparents were still being processed at the assembly camp, a furniture van pulled up outside what had been their home, and whatever remained was carted away. There was an oil painting of Lore and one of my father. Susy already had the matching painting of herself. I saw this lovely work in Klaus' home, but why would anyone outside of the family want these pictures? Klaus wanted them badly and almost left his hiding place to try and buy them back, a futile risk that Susy did not allow him to take. Everything was going to a special sale for newlyweds who could buy what they desired at a good discount, a real steal indeed. Did someone buy the painting of my father? Did it survive the war? Does some family have it on their wall? Compared with everything else, the loss of these objects is a small thing, but it remains, for me, an infuriating violation.

Before their stay at *Grosse Hamburger Strasse* was over, my grandparents were charged 250 Deutsche Marks for their "lodging," a room where twenty people were crammed together with no bathroom. On Thursday, January 28, 1943, a tram run by the Berlin Transport Company took them to the Anhalter Station, where they boarded transport I/87 with ninety-eight other elderly Jews. The train would carry them east through the cold, German landscape toward a destiny neither could have imagined.

CHAPTER SIX

THERESIENSTADT

THE FOWLER'S SNARE

My first glimpse of Theresienstadt came through the eyes of children. I was in college, planning my syllabus for an independent study in poetry therapy with a special focus on children. One day in the Brown University Bookstore, a bright yellow cover caught my eye. It belonged to the book *I Never Saw Another Butterfly: Children's Drawings and Poems from Terezin Concentration Camp, 1942-1944*. I don't know how long I stood there absorbed in reading it until I finally paid for it and brought the book back to my dorm. The fierce, artistic vitality of the children in that camp moved and inspired me. I wanted to find ways to support and nurture such creative power in other children, children in different yet difficult circumstances.

When Ana called me to read the Wikipedia article, and I saw that my grandparents had been taken to that very camp, I rushed to find the book I'd treasured since college and grasped it as a token of connection to them. Of all places, my own grandparents had been there, beginning in 1943, along with the very children who had opened my eyes thirty years ago. From that moment I longed to go there, to see where my grandparents had been, where my grandfather's ashes remained. When that day finally came, I couldn't go.

It was the eve of one of the most momentous days in my life, and I imagined preparing myself in prayer, perhaps meditating on the psalms of lament. Instead I lay in bed and watched junk TV. I had arrived in Prague a day early, my only chance to see the sights of that magnificent city. Touring Prague was not the purpose of my trip, but I was eager to fit in as much as possible as long as I was there. I decided to begin in the old Jewish quarter and was able to visit the Jewish Cemetery, dating from 1439, the Pinkas Synagogue, which has walls painted with the names of the 77,000 Czech Jews who perished under the Nazis, and what is called the Old-New Synagogue, in use since 1270. Then I went to a café and had some local Bohemian beer, sausage, and cabbage. After lunch, I was going to find a corner in one of the city's many churches and begin my prayer vigil, but I never made it to such a sanctuary.

I barely got back to my hotel before I began to be sick. At three in the morning, I was starting to realize that I might not be in any shape to travel as planned. By six, I knew that I could not. By eight, I was resolved that I would not leave Prague until I made the trip to Theresienstadt, no matter when that became possible. The hotel had the room available for me to stay another night, so I booked it.

I had no energy to read, so I alternated between sleep, bathroom bouts, and TV. There were a few talk shows, but the talk was all in Czech. There was cricket on CNN and a German version of the reality TV show *Hoarders*. Cricket made as little sense to me as the Czech-talking heads, so I was left with no other choice. Although my German is not good, it was easy enough to follow the show: the camera panning ceiling-high mounds of treasured trash, the distraught family, the earnest therapist—the Hoarder herself!

Glorious Prague was going on all around me. Others were out walking along the silvery Vltava River, across the Charles Bridge, visiting the fairytale castle, the gilded Baroque church of St. Nicholas, taking in rococo confections and Art Nouveau, deciding what traditional crafts to bring home and drinking in Wenceslas Square. I lay on my bed, waiting to get better, as sluggish as the TV hoarder. That night, I dreamed about my grandparents. Actually, the phrasing in Spanish is better—I dreamed with my grandparents. I felt they were with me throughout the night, but I couldn't remember any details.

* * *

The next day, with a supply of water, Coke, and a bag of dry crackers in my backpack, I headed for the bus that would take me to the town the Nazis publicized as "Hitler's gift to the Jews." We rode through the Bohemian countryside, passing tawny fields of corn and hops, the poppy-red roofs of distant villages, and pale, green hills edged with thick forests. If my grandparents had been able to see out their train window, this warm landscape was not what met their eyes, but rather a dull expanse, as uniformly brown as a storm trooper's shirt spread out over the hardened fields of winter. Did they really imagine they were being taken to a senior citizen's retirement home as they had been promised? By the end of the hour-long ride, my stomach was in knots, straining between the present and the past.

The bus stopped on the outskirts of Theresienstadt, a city originally built at the end of the eighteenth century by the Austrian emperor Joseph II as a fortification between the Elbe and Ohre Rivers. It was named for his mother, the archduchess and empress, Maria

Theresa. The construction had two parts, the main stronghold and what is now called the Little Fortress. Over time the main fortification was turned into a garrison town, and the Little Fortress was used as a prison.

When the Nazis invaded Czechoslovakia, they seized the Little Fortress to house their own political and military prisoners, many of whom were non-Jewish Czech communists. I decided to take a tour of this old fort before going into the town where my grandparents had been. There was time before the tour, so I wandered around the nearby cemetery where those prisoners whose bodies were found and identified at the end of the war are buried. Each stone had its own blossoming bush of red roses. No one was there except the gardener tending the bushes. I asked him if I might have a rose to take to the river for my grandfather when the time came. He kindly agreed on the spot and gave one to me.

As others got their cameras ready at the start of the tour, I stood holding my rose, bearing this sweet blossom through the gates of hell. We entered the prison under one of the *Arbeit Macht Frei* signs that hung over the gates of a number of camps, most famously Auschwitz. We saw rooms that held one hundred and fifty people, forty to a bed. I stared at the long wooden platforms used for beds and tried to figure out how forty people fit, but I simply couldn't imagine it. The prisoners slept without mattresses or blankets on the bare wood. There was one sink and one bucket of water, with one toilet per room. Those who were able to work received daily food rations at 5 am. Those who did not work got no food and soon starved to death.

While most of the prisoners were not Jewish, there were some who had been captured in resistance activities. The conditions they faced were worse than for the other prisoners. Jewish prisoners were kept, seventy at a time, in an old horse stable built for two horses. There was no toilet, no beds, and no room to lie down. A sign on the wall forbade speaking and smiling, as if anyone would be inclined to the latter. Jews were held for two to three weeks in this room and then sent to Auschwitz. None survived.

I could not image things getting worse in the Little Fortress, but our guide said that the nadir of prison life was to be found in the tiny solitary-confinement cells, where a person would be held in total darkness, with no food or water for ten days, or longer, until death. I was struck to learn that these cells were reserved for those considered the most dangerous criminals of all—writers and journalists, locked behind doors where not a trace of light from these torchbearers could escape.

And yet we know that there is no such thing as an impermeable wall. Physics tells us that what appears to be solid is mostly empty space and that what appears to be darkness is laden with invisible light. I am not a physicist, but I am intrigued by what quantum physics calls the "observation effect," which essentially says that the act of observation does not merely interpret reality but actually impacts it. According to one seminal experiment, an unobserved beam of electrons can behave as a mixture of waves and particles, yet when the beam is observed, the electrons behave only as particles or only as waves, depending on the type of measurement made, indicating that the very act of observation creates change, forcing the system into a single state. Therefore, though the writer may be confined to a cell, and his or her observations may go unpublished, the very act of their having seen and noted the truth matters. I am learning this on a more personal level as well. My father believed that his secret was tightly sealed away, yet waves and particles of light pass unhindered through our unconscious shadowland: "The light shines in the darkness, and the darkness doesn't extinguish the light" (John 1:5).

* * *

It was now time to approach the town where my grandparents arrived in January of 1943. The way there passed by an execution area and gallows set up outside the prison and then on to a swimming pool and beautiful apartments for the prison officers, guards, and their families. There were gardens, a tennis court, bowling alley, cinema, and kindergarten— all within earshot of the execution range. Our guide said that the pool was built by fourteen-year-old boys brought in from the town who worked by hand for three years and then were deported to their deaths as soon as the pool was finished.

This completed the Little Fortress tour of horrors. I had moved in a grim procession, bearing my rose, through spaces where suffering hangs in the air and evil is still palpable. I felt as though we, the visitors, were as ephemeral as ghosts, visiting the permanent dead. It was unthinkable that anyone would live there now, and eat, sleep, and raise their children or make love. The town below it is something else altogether.

The pocked and peeling concrete walls that surround the town in the shape of an eight-pointed star have grassy moss growing on top and are sinking into the ground, as if they would prefer to disappear from sight. Or perhaps because the dense weight of history pulls them under like a collapsing star. Before the Nazis arrived, Theresienstadt was home to about seven thousand Czech citizens and soldiers. On November 24, 1941, the town was taken over by the Gestapo. Jewish slave labor was used to refit the town for its new purpose, and by mid-1942, all of the residents were forced to leave. Unlike some camps, it was not built as a primary site for extermination. It was to be a prison camp for slave labor and, more importantly, a place to hold Jews for later transport to be killed elsewhere. By 1942 even a fast-paced murder-machine like Auschwitz could not keep up with the numbers of Europe's Jews marked for slaughter.

A large percentage of those deported to Theresienstadt were part of a Jewish intellectual and cultural elite, including doctors, scientists, musicians, and artists. There were also many children and elderly people like my grandparents. The Nazis promoted this concentration camp as a model ghetto. Although there was no systematized mass killing on site, thirty-five thousand died there from starvation, disease, and the camp's pervasively inhumane conditions. The rest perished when they were deported to other camps, mostly to Auschwitz. Of the 155,000 Jews taken to Theresienstadt, only about twelve thousand survived.

* * *

The train my grandparents boarded in Berlin stopped where the tracks ended at Bohusovice, a village about two miles from Theresienstadt. Five months later the tracks would be extended into the camp itself, through the labor of other inmates; but as it was, my grandparents had to get out and walk the two miles, carrying what was left of their luggage after being searched at *Grosse Hamburger Strasse*. I've seen drawings that depict long lines of elderly Jews, still in good traveling clothes, trudging down that road, bent under their bundles of hope. There is also a drawing of a funeral cart used to carry the frailest elderly into the camp, but I imagine that my proud grandparents were still capable of walking. One observer described "old men with well-trimmed white beards and mustaches, white-haired women with black hats, dresses, and gloves, walking sticks with silvery crooks, elegant suitcases as if they had come to a spa." This description mirrors photographic images of my grandparents in every detail.

A week before my grandparents arrived, an inmate of the camp wrote in his diary:

Winter has come, and with it a great chill. I remember how much we feared the winter. The situation is truly very bad. People are living in the attics where the temperature often falls below zero. Still more transports will be coming.

My grandparents must have been hit with full-on shock when their group reached the camp itself and they were herded at gunpoint, with shouted orders and barking dogs, into a dungeon-like underground intake area called *Die Schleuse* or "the sluice gate." Sluice gates are used in wastewater treatment plants to recover minerals in mining operations. In Theresienstadt, the Gestapo searched each deportee and removed anything deemed of value, including items like toothpaste and food. My grandparents, along with everyone else, then faced further interrogation and extensive paperwork. Processing at *Die Schleuse* could take days, during which the constant stream of those being treated as human waste had no toilet facilities and no place to lie down besides a cold floor strewn with wood shavings. My guess is that my grandfather's last hope bled out then and there, even though his heart would beat on for another four weeks.

According to a nurse who worked in *Die Schleuse*, what followed was a "horrible delousing procedure— hot showers followed by an hour-long wait in a cold room with only a light towel while their clothing was deloused." Many died of pneumonia, especially among the elderly and the children, but my grandparents made it through. Moritz was seventy-seven years old and Ida was seventy.

* * *

As I entered Theresienstadt, I first came to a building that now houses a museum with the Hebrew word *Zachor*, "Remember," over the doors. I went to the woman stationed at the front desk of the museum with a list of questions for which she had nothing but general answers. Her English level was better suited to giving directions to the bathroom than to helping me, and I could not speak her language. I'd come all this way longing to learn things that seemed to be slipping away at that desk. Before leaving New York, I had tried to arrange a meeting with someone who might have more detailed information concerning my family, but my emails prompted only a generic response. Now this gatekeeper of tourists and pilgrims was impatiently motioning for me to move aside so that she could attend to others. I had taken up more than my fair share of time, but in one final attempt to go beyond the limits of generalities, I took out a copy of the death certificate with my grandfather's name I'd brought. The woman paused and gestured for me to wait while she made a phone call. Soon I was on my way to see the director of the Theresienstadt archives, who was in his office and willing to meet with me.

He was kind and generous with his time and attention, and I was most thankful. He found a file on my grandmother that indicated she was *Haushalt,* which meant that she was "housebound" and not forced to work because of her age. He said that while it was obviously a good thing that she was not worked to death, her status also meant that she was not allowed much food. He told me that the *Haushalt* elderly had a high mortality rate from starvation. There was no similar record for my grandfather.

Based on the information in his files, he was able to show me on a map exactly where my grandparents had lived. Unlike many couples, they had been able to stay together until my grandfather was removed to the barracks for the sick. When Theresienstadt first opened, men and women were separated, as were the children, but by 1943, some couples were permitted to live together, perhaps to support the myth of humane conditions at the camp. I left with my map and set out to find the house where they spent the tragic *Lebensabend* of their marriage.

It was a long and eerie walk. The past is remembered in a former barracks, the crematorium, columbarium, mortuary, a secret Jewish prayer room, and sites such as the railway tracks that brought and took tens of thousands to their deaths. In between, one passes the shops, restaurants, and homes inhabited by today's residents, numbering around three thousand. These people were not much in view. I walked ten residential blocks without seeing anyone and felt like I was in an episode of the *Twilight Zone.* There were signs of human life—metal stands holding bags of garbage above the street and dingy shops with beer, cheeses, and canned goods for sale, but no evident customers. I also saw a few satellite dishes on flat rooftops, just above attics that were once crowded with prisoners without ventilation in the summer or heat in the winter.

Closer to the center of town, I saw some boys on their skateboards, a man walking his dog, and a teenage couple laughing and flirting. These are Czech citizens who needed a place to live and likely had little choice as to whether it was Theresienstadt or somewhere else. The young who live there today are busy making their own memories, but they are doing it in a space polluted by evil. For me, to walk through what was once a site of atrocity, now returned to function as a normal town, was a creepy experience.

I came to the street marked on my map and followed the numbers of the houses down to the end of the block. Most of the homes were painted in pastel colors and some had flowers in window boxes but not the house where my grandparents had stayed. It was in sad shape, by far the worst on the block, with chipped concrete and flaking paint. Like other homes in the town, it had been built for a single family, but after the Gentiles were evacuated, it was refitted to house the Jews who were too numerous for the barracks. Triple-decker wooden bunks were squeezed into every space possible, and when that was not sufficient, people were crammed into attics and basements.

This was how a town built for three thousand had grown to seven thousand before the Nazis took over and was then expanded to house more than fifty-five thousand people. Basically for every space intended for one, eighteen were squeezed in. Rooms built for four persons, would hold sixty. One writer describes the height of the crowding in this way: "If Berlin, for example, had had the same population density as Theresienstadt had in that month, the German capital would have contained nearly 100 million people or more than the combined population of Germany and Austria!"

Since there was no infrastructure to contend with so many people, the available plumbing for toilets and running water could not keep up with human need, causing many epidemics and deaths.

Newcomers like my grandparents brought their suitcases of clean clothes into spaces crawling with vermin and filled with the stench of people only allowed to bathe every other month and wash their clothing every three to four months. The conditions were worst in the attics where most of the elderly were sent immediately because they could not climb up into the bunk beds, while the bottom levels were already filled. There is no record to show if my grandparents were sent to the attic or not, just the house number. If so, there was no heat, and it was the end of January. Most winter mornings began with the removal of that night's stack of frozen bodies, more than a hundred and fifty a day from around the camp.

I had visited the site of Moritz's comfortable childhood home on Church Street in Wittmund and seen pictures of my grandmother's lovely home beside the brewery. I had seen their beloved villa and the stately house they retreated to after 1934, across from one of Lübeck's lush parks. I'd traveled to their address in Berlin's classy Grunewald neighborhood. But it was here, in a hellhole, that my grandparents spent their final days together. I wanted someone to stand with me and absorb this sadness, but the street was empty.

I saw a wild rose bush nearby and took one pink flower since I was saving my other rose for the river. I picked off the thorns as my grandmother had once done for me when I visited her as a child and left it on the windowsill of the ugly house, a rose of Sharon in the wasteland. I wonder if my grandmother's enduring gentleness, her instinctual desire to protect me from the slightest prick, was related to my father's own silence.

* * *

My grandfather endured for less than a month. At some point, he was taken to a barracks for the sick, visible from the house. The camp archivist had explained to me that each quarter of the camp was assigned to its own building for the sick since the main infirmary could not accommodate the many people falling ill, so I don't know if my grandmother was able to visit her husband there or if she ever saw him again.

The sick of Theresienstadt were tended by some of the best physicians in Europe, who were also inmates at the camp, but they were working in the worst of conditions, without necessary medicines. I learned from Klaus that Moritz had been taking blood-pressure medication on a daily basis at the time of his deportation. Without it, undergoing such trauma to body and soul, he may as well have been shot.

My grandfather survived in Theresienstadt for twenty-nine days. Dr. Ernst Freudenheim signed his death certificate, stating the time of death as 1:20 in the afternoon and the cause of death as pulmonary endema beacuse of a "ruptured heart." The official finding in Czech records correctly names his death as murder: "Murdered 25.02.1943 Terezín." Dr. Freudenheim himself was a Czechoslovakian Jew who had been an inmate at Theresienstadt since it opened. In January 1945, he was sent to Auschwitz and killed. Dr. Freudenheim was thirty-three years old.

My grandfather's body was taken to a mortuary that had a room for Jews and a room shared by Protestants and Roman Catholics. His death certificate lists his religion as "Evang." or Protestant. Some people were allowed to view their loved ones through glass in the mortuary, and services could be held. No records survive to tell if any religious service took place for Moritz that my grandmother might have attended. After the mortuary, his body traveled to the crematorium that had opened just five months before his death. Prior to that, the dead had been buried en masse in a field outside of town, but transporting the bodies there became inefficient as the numbers grew.

The crematorium was a stark room dominated by four furnaces able to cremate nearly two hundred bodies a day, four at a time. The ashes were searched for any gold and then put into individual cardboard boxes made by other inmates. Each box was labeled with the name and date of death and placed on shelves in the columbarium. This contributed to the belief that a proper burial would be possible after the war. I followed this *via dolorosa* to the mortuary, to the crematorium, and to the columbarium, silently, numbly saying my own prayers at each place.

∗ ∗ ∗

I wonder when my father got word of his father's death. By then he had been in the United States for almost five years. I don't know when or how my father heard anything. It would be two more years before he learned that his mother had survived. My father was close to his parents. He was Moritz's only and beloved son. He had been mentored and given extraordinary opportunities thanks to his father. As a child, I saw the tenderness between my father and his mother and their regular letters to each other.

At whatever point he learned the truth, my father's silence meant that he had to conceal his grief as well. There would be no formal rituals in synagogue or church, no sitting shiva, no community to hold him close and accompany him in his pain. No one in his vicinity could even acknowledge the loss, because he chose to hide it. My father went to work each day, sealing off whatever load of grief and guilt he had buried. When asked, he said that his father had died of a heart attack. I never knew my grandfather, but I find myself struggling to write about his final days, paralyzed at times with something different from writer's block. The words have become like heavy stones I try to hoist upon a grave that does not exactly exist. I do not have the tools that are needed, but I look into my grandfather's eyes, smiling at me in a photograph and push on.

***

My grandfather's death is much less surprising than my grandmother's survival for two years at Theresienstadt. Most people of her age did not survive. Starvation rations were intended to cause death among the weak in a matter of months. The distribution of food was overseen by the Council of Elders, Jewish leaders who were put in charge of many aspects of camp life. They faced a daily, impossible challenge—"arranging justice in a regime of injustice." Eventually they determined that an equal distribution of food could not work, and so it was decided that those who did hard labor and medical personnel would get the most calories, followed by the children, the regular workers, and last, the elderly.

My grandmother would have had to join the long lines with everyone else, standing for hours in heat or cold to get a small daily bread ration, a breakfast of ersatz coffee, a midday cup of watery soup with an occasional potato peel in it, and a final meal with more of the broth. The elderly usually got only half-portions. One survivor wrote about the soup as being made with leaves, dirt, and sand mixed in:

sometimes there was lentil soup for a change made from dried ground lentil pods, gray, tasteless, unappealing, stinking water without any nutritional value; normally we would throw it out disgustedly until we found regular takers for it: old people.

The more I learn, the more I wonder how my grandmother survived. Her rations did not provide enough calories or vitamins even for someone who was *Haushalt*. Did she ever get packages of food from the outside? Did people take pity on her? Those most likely to die right in the camp were elderly Germans from well-to-do backgrounds who did not work and who could not speak the operative language of the camp, which was Czech. A survivor from Prague described them:

Unattached and unassisted, they suffered from terrible hunger, which chased them out of their miserable attics, where they lived crowded with other old people covered with fleas, bedbugs and lice. They would wait patiently alongside the long queues during the distribution of watery soup. Although their clothes still betrayed a past elegance, they were unkempt and soiled. Most were emaciated and stooped, their faces could not hide their embarrassment. Moreover, they knew that they were no good at beggary . . . Still today, I can hear, ringing in my ears, their cultured German, as they asked those lined up their only question . . . "Nimmt der Herr die Suppe? oder die Dame?" "Could the gentleman or lady spare the soup?"

Ida must have possessed a rare internal strength.

* * *

To try to learn more of my grandmother's experiences over the two years she was at the camp, I searched online for survivors and found Inge Auerbacher living in Queens. It was easy to locate Inge because she lectures widely, has written a number of books, and has her own website. Her best-known book, *I Am a Star,* is for children and tells of her experiences at Theresienstadt from ages seven to ten. Of the fifteen thousand children sent to the camp, Inge is one of only one hundred and thirty-two known to have survived.

I wanted to take the train to Queens, but Inge insisted that she would come to my house. I fretted over what to serve her in my nonkosher kitchen. She told me not to worry, insisting that she would not want to eat anything. This didn't really answer my concern because I wanted to be as hospitable as possible. I finally went to a nearby Israeli restaurant and bought some hummus, falafel, labane, and pita bread. I also rode the despised ThyssenKrupp escalator down in the supermarket to get some disposable plates, just in case.

I opened my door to be hugged by a small, vivacious woman who ended up eating everything I served her, which made me happy. She was fine with the regular plates, which was good, as I'd forgotten to get paper cups for her tea. We were surprised to learn that she had lived on the very same block in Theresienstadt as my grandparents. Her family started out sleeping on the attic floor and then were able to move downstairs into a bed. She confirmed the intense crowding in every room of each house on the street.

With so many people, even neighbors did not necessarily know each other, but they did share many common experiences. Inge told me about one terrible day that my grandmother also endured. It was November 11, 1943, and the paranoid camp commandant,

Anton Burgur, ordered a census to be certain that everyone was accounted for. Inge remembers it as a cold and rainy day that began with everyone called outside very early in the morning. Forty-five thousand men, women, and children were made to march to a muddy field by a ravine surrounded by Czech soldiers toting machine guns. Inge recalls being terrified, especially when an SS officer slammed the butt of his gun into her mother's back. They had to stand in lines without moving all day and were given no food or drink. They had to satisfy their natural needs on the field without any privacy.

There were three groups doing the counting: the SS, the Czech guards, and the Council of Elders and Burgur would not allow it to end until each group came up with the same number, which was not happening. Inge recalls aching to sit down, but her mother held her up because to sit was to risk being taken out of line and shot. On the other hand, many people, especially the elderly, simply collapsed as the hours wore on, and were left where they fell. It grew colder as the sun set, and then it began to rain harder. Inge's thin clothes, and likely Ida's as well, were quickly soaked through as the counting continued. Finally, they were allowed to begin the muddy march back. By midnight, only half had made it, including Inge and her parents. Throughout the night, the rest were carried on stretchers, not a few directly to the morgue. Whether she walked or was carried, I don't know, but my grandmother survived the ordeal.

I wonder what went through her mind as she stood there or lay shivering on the muddy ground, what she thought about waiting in line for food or lying in her bed? Did she think about the life she and Moritz had built together? About her children and what was happening to them? Did she think back to her own Jewish girlhood in Zabrze? Did Hebrew songs rise in her heart? Did she pray in German? Did she curse God, or was the spark of faith smothered in the mud?

* * *

In the midst of such deeply dehumanizing circumstances there was a different and unique aspect to life in Theresienstadt that emerged from the treasury of intellectual and artistic gifts that passed through *Die Schleuse* miraculously intact. In hidden spaces and stolen moments, children were taught by former teachers, social workers, and artists. Inge recalls attending secret classes where she studied English and wrote poetry because of those who found energy, despite exhausting labor and hunger, to offer artistic outlets and inspiration to the many children among them.

Camp inmates also produced their own art and composed music, eventually being allowed to provide some public performances. A chorus of one hundred and fifty prisoners gave sixteen performances of Verdi's *Requiem* as a way of "singing to the Nazis what we cannot say to them." *Brundibár* was a children's opera first rehearsed in a Prague orphanage for Jewish children separated from their parents. When the Jewish composer, set designer, and most of the children were deported to Theresienstadt, they performed the opera there more than fifty times.

Others gave evening lectures on literature, philosophy, history, science, Judaism, and medicine, providing a respite, helping the audience of inmates to bear the unbearable. One composer, Viktor Ullmann, said: "By no means did we sit weeping by the rivers of Babylon. And our will to create was equal to our will to live."

I like to believe that my grandmother was among the throngs who found momentary relief in some of these events. She loved music, and it seems very probable to me that she would have found a way to attend at least a few of the concerts. With this in mind, I went to a performance at the 92nd Street Y featuring music composed and played at Theresienstadt. I closed my eyes and curled into the musical hammock with Oma, swaying and dreaming together in the dark until the strings left their final sigh in the air, and it was over.

* * *

The Nazis enthusiastically exploited the camp's artistic flowering for their own purposes. When the Red Cross insisted on visiting the camp after hearing rumors of mass extermination, the Nazis played the role of generous patrons of the arts and had an outdoor pavilion and lecture hall built in the center of town. New musical instruments were brought in. It was part of a macabre theatrical production that included freshly painted buildings, a state-of-the-art playground, faux cafes and stores, and new clothing and extra food for those who were compelled to play the part of happy camp residents.

In order to reduce the camp's population, thousands of inmates were sent to their deaths at Auschwitz prior to the visit. A few rooms were enlarged and set up to hold three or four specially selected and prepared inmate actors. The elderly and sick who were not deported had to remain out of sight. It occurs to me that my grandmother was fortunate to have lived on the edge of the town because those buildings would not be part of the charade, and those who lived there were left alone. The day before the visit, women were forced to scrub the sidewalks with their hairbrushes. Some of the children were going to perform *Bundibár* for the Red Cross with new sets and costumes that had been provided. Inge told me that she begged her mother to join in, but her mother said that you should never volunteer for anything because you don't know what the outcome will be.

The Red Cross visitors arrived, and some scarcely left their cars. They returned with glowing reports of excellent food, medical care, and even stylish clothing. The children who had been in the opera were quickly sent to their deaths. It's hard to understand why the Red Cross would allow the Nazis such tight control over their visit. It makes no sense at all. Emboldened by this propaganda coup, the Nazis went on to make a movie about this model town and their wonderful treatment of Jewish residents.

Eight months later, in February of 1945 my grandmother made a decision that probably saved her life. When I first spoke with my relatives in Australia to find out what they knew of my grandmother's time in Theresienstadt, they could tell me nothing except the story of her liberation. They told me that by the beginning of 1945, she was utterly worn down. While others did anything possible to avoid transports to the East, she was ready to go and end her misery.

The story had come to Uli through his wife, Ursula, who was one of Susy's children and my cousin. Before her death, Ursula had talked about this at some point with Uli, who passed it on to me.

What I know from the historical account is that every transport to the East was feared. Inge told me that it was something you didn't ever want to think about, but of course, people constantly worried. According to one account, "The ever-present threat of deportation to the East dominated life in Theresienstadt; it hung over everybody day and night." The fear grew worse in January of 1945 when a transport arrived with some who knew directly of people being gassed.

Before each transport, the Council of Elders had the horrible task of making a selection. Then something new was presented in February of 1945. People could sign up to go on a transport that would take them to Switzerland and freedom! Where one might expect a stampede of eager prisoners, there were none because who would believe such a preposterous tale? It was made even more absurd given that gas chambers were then being built for use right at Theresienstadt. Why would those who were constantly plotting your demise grant you a ticket to freedom?

As happened for other transports, people had to report to an area where the lists of deportees were prepared. This time you could volunteer, but there was still a selection from among those who did. The version I heard when I first phoned Uli in Australia is that my grandmother came forward to take the place of a mother who had volunteered with her son only to find that she was chosen to leave, while he had to stay behind. I was told that my grandmother stepped in and requested to take this mother's place, expecting to go to her death.

So why did the Nazis allow their prey to board a freedom train? The former president of Switzerland, Jean Marie Musy, came to fear repercussions for his pro-Nazi leanings when he realized that he might be on the losing side of the war. He worked to get one Jewish couple in France released, and word of this spread to the Orthodox Rabbinical Association of America, who wanted to see if he could negotiate the release of more Jews. Musy went to Himmler who agreed to allow for a transport of Jews to leave Theresienstadt and go to Switzerland after a million dollars was deposited into a Swiss bank account in his name. It was to be the first of many such deals, but when Hitler discovered the plan, he put a stop to it. The transport in

February of twelve hundred inmates from Theresienstadt would not be repeated.

Once aboard this freedom train, the fairy tale came to life. Everyone was given better suitcases, shoes, and clothing. They received bread, sugar, sausages, and Ovaltine. Even then, there were doubts. One passenger on that train, Gerda Haas, wrote a book of her experiences in which she recalls, "[we] watched anxiously, observing and arguing with one another as to which direction the train traveled at any given time—was it headed East toward Poland and the extermination camps? Or was it turning West?"

The journey lasted three days, and as they drew closer to Switzerland, the women got lipstick and other cosmetics to make them appear as healthy as possible. Heading for death, my grandmother stepped into a new beginning in a new country where she would live for another twenty-two years. Just a decade later, she would hold me in her arms, grown soft and round again, but I was too little to remember that first visit when I was eighteen months old.

Did it matter that she boarded the train, given that the camp was liberated only three months later? I think it did. In an effort to cover up their atrocities, the Germans began evacuating other camps and sending a large influx of inmates to Theresienstadt. This led to an epidemic of typhus that decimated the town. Even after liberation arrived on May 8, 1945, the entire area was quarantined, as hundreds continued to die. By then my grandmother was inhaling the fresh Swiss air.

I wonder now about my own name. My mother wanted to call me Penelope, although she didn't like the nickname Penny. My father convinced her that Heidi would be better. I liked my name, even though the only other Heidi I knew as a child was a neighbor's

German shepherd. Also, people would frequently remark on "the book about you," much to my annoyance (although I loved the book). Was my naming a way for my father to draw his mother and daughter together? It seems that her survival in the shelter of the Swiss Alps and my birth intersected in his heart.

* * *

Did my grandmother ever discuss her experiences in Theresien-stadt with her three children—my father, Susy, and Lore? Whatever she might have said is lost except for what I learned from Uli: she felt that she could not go on, and then, she was saved. There was nothing about Oma that indicated anything of her suffering. Her eyes were warm and untroubled, and in them I saw only her love. I remember visits when I was four, eight, and eleven years old filled with long Alpine walks and sweet treats. Even though I saw her infrequently, I felt as close to her as I did to my grandmother in New Jersey. There was always a postcard to me from Oma within reach. I displayed the most recent one on my dresser and kept the rest in a special box. Letters she wrote to my parents were read aloud in translation by my father in the evening, often after dinner in the glow of candles set in his heirloom silver candlesticks. We welcomed this grandmother to our table like an invisible Sabbath queen. An ocean of distance did nothing to dim the brightness of her presence in our lives.

Oma died close to my thirteenth birthday, for which she'd sent me a gift—a silver heart necklace with a single pearl cradled inside the curves of the heart. I treasure the necklace, but her real legacy to me is in how she lived in the aftermath of trauma, as though she'd plucked every thorn of bitterness from her flesh.

MOSES AT THE RIVER

When you pass through the waters, I will be with you;
when through the rivers, they won't sweep over you.

—Isaiah 43:1b-2a

Just as the Egyptian pharaoh twisted the life-giving power of the Nile River into a deathbed for Jewish children, the Nazis used the Ohre River to bury their crimes. From the time I learned of my grandfather's fate, I felt pulled by a tide of longing toward the Ohre River. If I could not touch my grandfather, I yearned to feel the water that cradled the ash of his bones. Before that could happen, I wanted an immediate connection and decided that I would get a tattoo. I don't even have pierced ears, but I suddenly wanted a tattoo with his number on my arm. I did not reflect on the offense that this could cause. I was thinking only of a solidarity that would allow me to see, daily, in my skin, the truth that had been kept from me. I wanted to carry a visible mark that could not be erased, to bear the unseemly sign of that truth in my body where it could never leave me again.

I soon discovered that neither of my grandparents had such a tattoo. In order to foster the illusion that they were not branded and bound for slaughter, the inmates of Theresienstadt were not tattooed. Instead, they were made to wear metal badges with their number. When I learned this, I thought of getting a tattoo of a star or of Mortiz's Jewish name, Moses Lazarus, but at the time of this writing, my skin remains unmarked. I've chosen this other, painstaking imposition of ink upon the page, piercing memory, mind, and heart.

I followed my map out of town along the river. It was a long walk and that turned out to be a good thing for me since few people make the trip, and I preferred to be alone. I saw that there was a very high bank perpendicular to the river and no way that I would be able to climb down. The water I longed to touch was beyond reach. I began to resign myself to this huge disappointment, not wanting to spoil a pilgrimage that was more about honoring my grandfather than any other desire. At least I could drop my iron pellet from the *Hochofenwerke* and toss my rose upon the waters. I could pray. I could be near.

In the distance, I saw a tall monument. It was a sculpture of a weeping woman wrapped in a gown of grieving faces. I approached and read the plaque: "At this place in November 1944, the ashes of twenty-two thousand Jewish victims from the Terezin ghetto were ordered by the Nazis to be thrown into the Ohre River." Then I turned and saw the steps leading down to the river's edge. Those who planned this memorial understood the need to descend to the water, and I was grateful. The stairway was narrow, with a space at the bottom just big enough for one person. I was relieved to be alone to do as I wished and to stay as long as I wanted.

I had considered saying Kaddish. Wouldn't my grandfather's devoutly Jewish parents have wanted Kaddish said for their son? Perhaps they would, but I was dissuaded by the rabbi of Ansche Chesed, the congregation down the street from my church, who said it was not appropriate for me to do this. I had also thought about a Lutheran memorial service. The problem was that I wanted to do what would be meaningful for my grandfather, and I didn't know what that would be. Although my grandparents had their three children baptized, I don't know if they themselves truly converted. I don't know what faith, if any, lit up the hidden corners of their souls when evil came crashing down around them. Was my grandfather's faith extinguished in the sluice-gate? Was his Judaism a dimly burning wick?

Part of me wanted to scream because of the ashes beneath the water, the sodden bone meal of old people and children mingled in the mud, but I did not allow myself to scream. I wanted to bear a spirit of reverence where none had been. I found my foothold where I often do, in the prayer book that Jews and Christians hold in common, the psalms. I prayed a number of psalms which actually open into screams. I emptied my heart of psalms and I read Isaiah aloud:

> Don't fear, for I have redeemed you;
> I have called you by name; you are mine.
> When you pass through the waters, I will be with you;
> when through the rivers, they won't sweep over you.
> When you walk through the fire, you won't be scorched
> and flame won't burn you. (Isaiah 43:1b-2)

Under the weeping willows, an ancestral Kaddish rippled across the water. I sang some alleluias and remember little else. Then I threw the iron out into the water and set the rose afloat on my grand-father's quavering grave, sixty-seven years late. A light wind brushed my hair. A bird called out to unseen companions. I ran my hand through the water one last time.

CHAPTER SEVEN

POST-WAR

RECONSTRUCTION

The Theresienstadt memorial areas and the commemorative site by the river were not opened until more than a decade after my father's death. I wonder if he ever allowed himself to consider the question of what had become of his father's remains. Only now, in writing this book, have I come to understand what feels like a part of his response. Both of my parents were active in our church, although my mother had more time for volunteer work. There were only two volunteer activities that I recall being of great importance to my father: the church's burial society and the development of affordable housing for the elderly of Summit, where we lived. For several years, my father went to numerous meetings as he took on the issue of housing for Summit's low-income elderly with great passion and ultimate success.

His interest in the burial society grew in response to the problem of grieving families being taken advantage of in the process of making arrangements with funeral homes. My mother became aware of this through her role on the worship and music committee. She and my father organized a small group with the pastor's support and met with a local funeral home director to ensure that people were treated fairly and that all options, including cremation and plain, inexpensive coffins, were made readily available. They worked with the pastor to present educational events on burial practices and options for the congregation.

At the time, my father's sudden interest in burial issues seemed out of character because I had gotten the message early on that he didn't like to discuss such things. I remember driving with my parents on the Brooklyn-Queens Expressway on our way to visit Aunt Lore when I was around four years old. There is an expansive stretch of cemeteries on both sides of the highway, and I asked about it. My parents explained that people who died were buried in the ground there and the stones marked each person's grave. After a time of meditative silence, my voice piped up from the back seat: "When I die, you can pickle me and put me in a jar by the fireplace so you can see me." We almost did die right then as my shocked father struggled to keep control of the wheel. "Pickled!" he gasped, "Where did she learn about pickled?"

Earlier that week, my mother and I had visited the Trailside Nature Museum in Watchung, New Jersey, which featured row upon row of animal specimens floating in glass jars, reminding me of pickles. I can distinctly remember my mother trying to hurry me on to something else, but I wanted to take my time with each fascinating jar. If there was any other type of exhibit on display, I can't remember it. The new and improved facility is now called the Trailside Nature and Science Museum. I took the virtual tour on their website and it appears that today's children are not treated to jars of pickled animals.

* * *

I can imagine that the church's conversation around cremation held particular interest for my father. For most Jews, cremation is considered to be a desecration of the body compounded with reminders of the Shoah. Some people, Jews and Christians, fear or believe that cremation has an impact on afterlife and resurrection. I imagine that it was helpful for my father to hear that the state of the physical body at death and in burial does not shape the body of resurrection. St. Paul describes it like this: "What is sown is perishable, what is raised is imperishable. It is sown in dishonor, it is raised in glory. It is sown in weakness, it is raised in power. It is sown a physical body, it is raised a spiritual body" (1 Corinthians 15:42a-44a NRSV). The burial society led the congregation in creating the Garden of Resurrection for cremains on the church property. Both of my parents chose to be buried there among the rose bushes. I remember each time, carrying the box of remains outside after the service, pouring them into the prepared holes and covering them over, watering the dirt with my tears.

I don't think it was conscious, but I am convinced that my father gravitated toward the two issues of affordable housing for the elderly and burial practices because they provided a way to answer his helplessness and guilt over what he had not been able to do for his own elderly parents when they were taken to Theresienstadt.

* * *

The Germans have a word for the process of trying to come to terms with the past. To a non-German speaker, it appears as long and bewildering as the journey itself, *Vergangenheitsbewältigung,* which breaks down into *Vergangenheit,* meaning "the past" and

Bewältigung or "to deal with or to cope with something." This is the word most often used in Germany to name the process of facing up to the Shoah. It has been in use since the late 1950s, when the immediacy of postwar reconstruction was underway and the harder work of laying a new moral foundation began.

I've come to see that my father's own reconstruction project was focused on 57 Club Drive in Summit, New Jersey. He and my mother worked with an architect to design the house where he lived for thirty years until his final days in intensive care. I think that for him our home was built to safeguard the future from the past, or more specifically, from the painful past. Vera Schiff, a survivor of Theresienstadt writes in her memoir: "We tacitly embarked on a conspiracy of silence . . . .We hoped that our children would grow up happier and would be better adjusted if they were not exposed to the truth of our history." I believe my father's hopes were the same.

I've saved a crayon drawing from when I was four or five. It's been framed and hanging on our bedroom wall for years. I am in a blue dress, sitting on a swing stationed between two tall, solid trees. My arms stretch out towards the thick, brown trunks that have matching green circles on top, like heads. Before, I simply saw myself enjoying our backyard swing. Now, I see a child, safe and secure between her parents, unshakably rooted. But that is not all, and that is not what led me to save and frame the drawing. In the blue air above my head, between the trees, are bells, five of them floating at jaunty angles, their colorful clappers ringing for joy. This is the foundation my parents gave me, and my father likely believed that knowing a fuller, shadowed truth would serve no good purpose. Since he never told my mother, he probably believed the same thing about his marriage. Why spoil something so lovely?

I wonder when would have been the right time for my father to break his silence? My parents considered me to be an oversensitive child. I was not allowed to watch *Lassie* because it was not good to cry right before bedtime. I'd beg and promise not to cry, but the mournful music at the end never failed to induce tears and that was that. My mother was as concerned about protecting me as my father. For most of my life, I knew her as a strong, capable woman who carried on no matter what— even when living with Parkinsons. But when she was a young bride, it was a bit different. Because of my father's age, they wanted to have a baby as soon as possible. I was born eleven months after their wedding, and my mother almost hemorrhaged to death. She came home and was listless and ill for many months. She also began to suffer from terrible headaches, which lasted until I was six and began to get them, too. My mother later told me that the pediatrician said my headaches might be caused in response to her own, and so she willed herself to stop getting them. I never knew my mother to suffer another headache for the rest of her life. The lesson I learned is that you protect those you love from pain when possible and then use your strength to help others. We were the helpers, not the victims. When I was sickly as a teenager with toxoplasmosis, my parents' protective instincts went into overdrive. I needed to be careful. I should not be upset. Every single letter that I received in college from my father cautioned me to be sure to take care of myself because I was no good to anybody else if I didn't.

However, there was also the powerful message that we were meant to do good. I was protected but never encouraged to live in a cocoon. I grew up with the sense that my life was meant to make the world a better place in some way. My moves outward, to the rural poverty of Johns Island, to Argentina for a year of seminary and human-rights work, and to the South Bronx for nineteen years of pastoral ministry and community organizing were all accompanied by parental worry but also unremitting support, pride, and encouragement. To arrive on the banks of the Ohre River felt like a natural consequence of that journey. Unwittingly, my father led me there.

✳ ✳ ✳

The Gospel of John records the following story of Jesus healing a man born blind:

> "While I am in the world, I am the light of the world." After he said this, he spit on the ground, made mud with the saliva, and smeared the mud on the man's eyes. Jesus said to him, "Go, wash in the pool of Siloam" (this word means sent). So the man went away and washed. When he returned, he could see. (John 9:5-7)

John's contemporaries may have appreciated the healing properties of saliva and mud, but for most of us today, a paste of spit and dirt is the last thing we would want rubbed onto our eyes. And yet, it seems to me that this is part of the process of enlightened vision and action. Smearing the mud of reality over our eyes, however foul and distasteful it may be, is the beginning step in coming to see where we have been and where we need to go.

Edzard has been a singularly determined force for *Vergangenheitsbewältigung* in Wittmund, opening the eyes of his town to the past. Without his efforts, I would have never been acquainted with much of my own history. The work of *Vergangenheitsbewältigun* is long and still in process. Facing a hideous reality, one which beggars the thesaurus of evil in any effort to describe it, and changing in response—the turning toward and then turning around that is the root of repentance, accepting that nothing is ever enough because there is no remedy, yet figuring out a way forward—this work is necessarily incomplete. Our repairs are ever inadequate, and so there is always more to do. My father's hometown city of Lübeck is an example of this. I have always felt a special bond with Lübeck because of my father, our visits there, and because I grew up surrounded by a virtual-reality version of the city brought into our home through artwork and artifacts. Lübeck is a part of me, and now I see that Lübeck is still coming to terms with itself, as I am. It's where I returned when I left Theresienstadt.

AFTER YEARS OF FORGETTING

When Hans and I visited Lübeck the year before this solo trip, I was struck by the many belated recognitions of my grandfather. In the 1980s, there was a flurry of remembrance that resulted in a book about the ironworks, an exhibition at the St. Anne's Museum, an oil painting of Moritz in the Burgkloster Museum, the 1985 opening of the Industrial Museum and History Workshop of Herrenwyk, and even a nearby street named for him, the *Mortiz-Neumark Strasse*. For years, it was as though my grandfather had not existed and now the city that cast him out decided to welcome him home.

Before this trip to Lübeck, my family in Australia sent me a newspaper clipping with the headline, "After Years of Forgetting, the City Honors Moritz Neumark." It was dated May 29, 1986, and the honor referred to is a bronze memorial plaque in Lübeck's *Rathaus* (City Hall). The plaque had the names of seven Jewish city senate members murdered by the Nazis, but my grandfather's name was not among them. The article explained that until the book about the iron works was published in 1985, "his fate was unknown." Renate had some letters saved that included one addressed to her and to Lore from the St. Anne's Museum. In preparation for their exhibition, the curator requested family photographs and information including the question, "*Wann und wo ist er gestorben?*" The German was simple enough for me to understand ("When and where did he die?"), but I kept rereading it because I found it so hard to believe. Was it possible that they really didn't know the answer?

It's true that my grandparents were deported from Berlin rather than from Lübeck, but it was no secret that the Nazis had identified them as Jews, which was why my grandfather was removed from his home, the iron works, and all of his civic positions. Did the city believe its own paper's earlier propaganda that he'd gone off into a "lovely" retirement? The entire iron works' records were in the city archives and included the information about my grandparents' fate. Perhaps the curator did not know where to turn, but what about those who did research for the original plaque? How is it that they had unearthed information about the other murdered Jews but nothing about Moritz, a man of particular prominence for Lübeck? Some that I have spoken with believe that his name was left off because of a convenient case of civic amnesia. What was done to my grandfather may have been too shameful for the town fathers to admit.

Thankfully, the process of *Vergangenheitsbewältigung* continues, and when the city council became aware of the omission in 1985, they insisted that the memorial plaque be altered to reflect the truth. The bronze piece was cut in half and a new section was inserted with my grandfather's name before it was soldered back together. Today, the memorial is mounted just outside the doors into the city senate chambers. After the list of names, it reads: "Their death is a constant admonition to us."

* * *

About six months before this trip, I was surprised to get a phone call from one of the pastors at St. Mary's in Lübeck. Pastor Ina von Kortzfleisch-Brinkmann knew of my work as a Lutheran pastor engaged in urban ministry through a friend of a German student like Carsten, who'd worked with me in the Bronx. Ina was contacting me about visiting my church in New York during her upcoming sabbatical. She knew nothing of my own ties to her city and church. As we talked and I told her that I was planning to visit Lübeck, she invited me to stay in her home. Unbeknownst to me, she alerted others to my visit including the mayor of Lübeck, Bernd Saxe. He saw this as a unique opportunity to address the past and arranged a reception for me with a mix of city officials, church leaders, church historians, and scholars of the Nazi period.

We gathered around a polished mahogany table in the *Rathaus*, with coffee, cookies, and marzipan. Mayor Saxe made introductions and invited me to share about my family research and writing project. Then, he began to speak about my grandfather: "He was an important man and this city knows what he did for us." Bernd Saxe looked into my eyes and expressed his sorrow and remorse over what the city he now served had done and had failed to do. It was the summer of 2010, seventy-six years after Moritz was betrayed by those who sat a few rooms away from where we met and voted that he would henceforth be forbidden to set foot in the company he built. They had already booted him out of their midst months earlier. Bernd Saxe's words could not undo the ruinous trajectory of the past, but they still mattered immensely.

The same is true of the work of a few church historians and theologians who were also at the table and who gave me some of the research they have done on the churches of Lübeck during the Nazi era and postwar aftermath. The first official reaction after the war showed no contrition or even recognition of what happened to the Jews of Lübeck. It was simply noted that "they left," like my grandfather going on to "retirement." As was true throughout Germany, there was more anger over how the Nazis had damaged the church as an institution than repentance over Jewish genocide. Even Helmut Thielicke blamed the Third Reich's ascendancy on a spirit of secularity rather than on anti-Semitism. Others justified themselves by claiming that the Nazi juggernaut was too powerful to counter in any effective way.

Pastor Martin Niemoeller was one who did speak out with deep regret for not doing enough. He accepted both personal blame and spoke to the guilt of the church, as did Karl Barth, but this was rare. Ten years after the war, Bishop Balzer was able to receive his full pension and live comfortably in Hamburg until his death in 1975. In Lübeck a pastor was appointed for Jewish Christians who arrived as war refugees so they might have "separate but equal" worship. Until 1977 the churches of Lübeck had an "Israel Sunday" with a special offering for mission to Jews. Even then, the only good Jew was a baptized Jew.

It was not until the late 1980s and 1990s that critical research and reflection took shape, and in 2001, the Burgkloster Museum opened an exhibition about the history of Jews in Lübeck. At the same time, members of congregations gathered for a program on the historical and theological roots of anti-Semitism in the churches.

The need to face these realities remains an ongoing challenge. Pastor Kortzfleisch-Brinkmann told me that St. Mary's has an area with names and photos of all clergy from the church minus one. To this day, Bishop Balzer does not appear—not, she notes, because he debased his calling, but because it is unpleasant to think about.

The day after meeting in the *Rathaus* was Sunday, and Pastor Kortzfleisch-Brinkmann had invited me to preach at St. Mary's. This was something I could never have imagined. At first, I wanted to decline the invitation which came on Friday and gave me far too little time to prepare for what felt like an overwhelming challenge. On the other hand, it seemed rude to refuse my host's generous offer. It was also a once-in-a-lifetime chance to stand and speak in a place so central to my family's history of silence. It was an opportunity to speak words of life in a pulpit that had been used to promote death during the Third Reich. I'm often struck that the physical brutality all too frequently visited upon queer youth begins in the pulpit. It may not be sanctioned by most preachers; however, once you link a person's orientation to the devil, it's easy to go on to demonize and dehumanize that person to the point that the violence is easily justified by those who enact it.

Ina told me that I should be prepared to know that the congregation included some former Nazis and Nazi sympathizers who may or may not be present. I wasn't sure what it meant to be prepared for Nazis, but I decided that I would preach the same way whether or not they were there. I told the congregation that in 1953, when my father brought my mother to the church on their honeymoon, they never would have dreamed that nearly six decades later, their daughter would stand to preach in this very pulpit. I told them about my father's love for their church and how he kept his confirmation certificate from 1918 on his bedroom wall. This was true, but although I put on the black robe I was given to wear and the startlingly large, starched, ruffled collar (seen in sixteenth-century paintings of Queen Elizabeth and out-of-fashion for centuries except among clergy in North German cities like Lübeck), I did not want to don the role of proud granddaughter of the church. Once, I would have done so happily, but that was before I understood the fuller ramifications of the silenced bells and before I knew about the murderous speech that had regularly emanated from that very pulpit.

I did not select the texts from which I would preach. They were part of a lectionary used by all the Lutheran churches in Germany. The gospel for that Sunday was a story from Saint Luke where Jesus talks about party invitations:

> Then Jesus said to the person who had invited him, "When you host a lunch or dinner, don't invite your friends, your brothers and sisters, your relatives, or rich neighbors. If you do, they will invite you in return and that will be your reward. Instead, when you give a banquet, invite the poor, crippled, lame, and blind. And you will be blessed because they can't repay you. Instead, you will be repaid when the just are resurrected." (Luke 14:12-14)

I reflected on my grandfather who gave his city industrial power, jobs, homes, electricity and was host and guest at many a party, until all was taken away and he and my grandmother were alone. Yet not utterly alone. There was another reading:

> Let mutual love continue. Do not neglect to show hospitality to strangers, for by doing that, some have entertained angels without knowing it. Remember those who are in prison, as

though you were in prison with them; those who are being tortured, as though you yourselves were being tortured. (Hebrews 13:1-3 NRSV)

This text from Hebrews describes our calling not only to invite those who are often unwelcome, but to position ourselves alongside of those who are suffering. It points to the example of Jesus, another Jew rejected, arrested, and taken outside the city gate to be tortured and murdered. Tragically, it points to what was the abject failure of the church—and to what remains the only way forward. "We must always take sides," says Elie Wiesel, "Neutrality helps the oppressor, never the victim. Silence encourages the tormentor, never the tormented."

I could see Renate sitting in the front of the church, wiping tears from her eyes as I spoke. If there were Nazis present, none of them had anything to say to me, but others were appreciative, and I remember one woman in particular. She told me that her mother had been confirmed in the church like my father, and then she broke down. She quickly gathered herself and added that her mother was a Nazi perpetrator and that she has hated her for forty years, since she was ten years old. She also expressed shame, a hand-me-down cloak that can come to feel like a second skin. This woman wore it religiously to church. Then she told me that I had helped her. I couldn't imagine how that might be true until she said that I had mentioned the unmentionable. In forty years, this woman had never heard anything spoken directly from the pulpit about the Nazi era, but she needed to hear it because it was an awful part of the self she brought to St. Mary's.

Sadly, many people could add items to a long list of "Things Not Fit to Mention in Church." There are churches today where it is not safe to talk about racism and White supremacy, about being infected with HIV/AIDS, not safe to speak about incest and other forms of sexual violence, addictions that may be addressed by 12-step groups in the church basement but not in the sanctuary, depression, and mental illness to name a few examples. Never mentioning such real struggles in the lives of those who come to hear a word of hope is a shaming act in itself. The implicit message is that your truth is so loathsome we can't even talk about it here. There are people who think preaching is an outmoded form of communication, but I believe it can still make a difference for good or for evil.

When I was a pastor in the South Bronx, my congregation taught me about no-holds-barred honesty in church. I remember one woman who used to pray: "I thank you Lord for my psychiatric medication that keeps me out of the hospital. I thank you Lord for my HIV medication that keeps me alive." These life-giving advances in modern medicine are well worth giving thanks for, but such prayers would shock in most mainline churches.

Sweeping our mess under the carpet doesn't help. We need more spit and dirt in our churches because God still uses spit and dirt to heal our blinding hatreds and fears. This is why I keep a photograph of St. Mary's broken bells by my desk, reminding me that there must be a place in the church for our brokenness, a place for naming the suffering and injustices that many would like to forget about despite the reality that many more can never forget.

After leaving St. Mary's, Renate took me to Niederegger for brunch. Over eggs and smoked salmon, she told me how amazing it was to hear about her family from the pulpit and how difficult it was for her to know that my father had kept silent all of his life. She looked at me across the table and told me I have my Oma's eyes. I guess my father did as well, which is why I am told I have his eyes.

Renate then spoke again of her own long-lost dreams. Sometimes, the Pool of Siloam where we go to wash the mudpack from our eyes is filled with tears.

A Good Star

You set a table for me
right in front of my enemies.

—Psalm 23:5

My flight home was leaving from Hamburg where Klaus' daughter Susy lived. We met and went on a long walk by the Alster Lake, catching up on our present lives. Then we turned to the past. Klaus had told me about life in Berlin in the weeks and months at the end of the war, and young Susy filled me in further based on stories from her namesake and grandmother, my father's sister Susy, who lived in Brazil for many years with Klaus and his family.

In late April of 1945, the Russian army stormed into Berlin for the final battle of the war, a million troops on a mission to avenge ethnic hatred with ethnic hatred. Just as Hitler ultimately branded all Jews as one, the Russians made no distinction between types of Germans. Berlin hospitals estimated that between 95,000 and 130,000 women were raped over the course of two months. After reading the anonymous memoir about these rapes, *A Woman in Berlin, Eight Weeks in a Conquered City*, I wondered what had happened to Aunt Susy and my cousin Ursula. The fighting was focused in the city center, and they lived on the outskirts, but there, too, the Red Army came seeking food, drink, shelter, and women.

It was only a matter of time before the Russians arrived at Susy's door. At first, a commander came asking for water. Surprisingly he warned Susy that he could not control his soldiers who would arrive any day and that she should hide everything of value. Klaus had a box of very good French cognac that was once a gift from my grandfather. They took it into the basement with some neighbors and drank it all. Klaus remembers being very sick and not wanting ever to drink cognac again.

Ursula remained successfully hidden in the coal cellar, occasionally coming out for air on the flat roof at night, but that became too dangerous when the Russian soldiers arrived and camped out in every room of the house. Ursula remained in the small, dark space for weeks. Her daughter Barbara in Australia told me that Ursula spoke of coming out after the soldiers had departed and finding their home wrecked and befouled by feces, vomit, and blood. Her friends, three girls who lived next door, had all committed suicide right before the Russians arrived at their house. Such suicides were not uncommon. According to Klaus, when I asked him about it, Susy survived without being raped.

A year later, I met Klaus in Connecticut, where an old friend he knows from a labor camp now lives. Erika paid for Klaus to come from Brazil to visit her as a ninetieth-birthday gift. She invited me and my husband for afternoon coffee, and so we drove to Greenwich from Manhattan. The table was formally set with silver, embroidered linens and a spread of cakes, fruit and whipped cream. It was very German. At one point, Gregorio accompanied Erika into the kitchen to get something. Klaus seemed to be staring into space, and I asked him what he was thinking. He told me then that the Russians raped his mother. Silence is not always broken all at once. Some words are so heavy that it takes many attempts to haul them up to the surface.

✳ ✳ ✳

When the battle of Berlin brought the war to an end, food was extremely scarce and to get anywhere people had to make their way through the rubble of six-hundred thousand homes and countless other buildings. Klaus, who seemed to have a knack for doing well in any circumstance, took his photographic equipment and was let into the clubs where U.S. military personnel ate and danced the night away. He took pictures of the soldiers and their partners and was able to provide an unbeatable overnight turnaround service. The coal cellar where Ursula hid was now his dark room. Klaus was allowed to bring his sister and brother along as his assistants, and the soldiers gave them food to eat on site and tins of used frying oil and tea bags as well as powered eggs to take home. In addition, Klaus was paid for the photographs in the currency of the day, cigarettes worth ten marks apiece. While others could barely find enough to eat, Klaus' enterprise kept his family from hunger.

My aunt Susy responded by cooking whatever she had, every day, and feeding all who came, without questions, usually fifty to a hundred persons. Years later, Susy would visit Europe for months at a time, never staying at a hotel or paying for meals. My mother always marveled at Susy's many generous friends. Now I understand. As her granddaughter told me, "For the rest of their lives, the people she fed during that time in Berlin could never do enough for her."

I think about the fact that Susy, who never denied her Jewish roots and had close Jewish friends, was very likely feeding the enemy, providing essential nourishment to people who may gladly have turned her over to the Nazis. I don't believe that she did this with a view to avoiding future hotel bills.

Klaus soon moved to Brazil, and Peter went to Venezuela. Ursula married and emigrated to Australia. Susy would soon follow Klaus to Brazil, where she lived for twenty-five years until moving near the end of her life to be with Ursula. Three days before her death in 1979, Susy dictated a letter to Ursula for the family that included the following lines:

> Difficult times and grave worries accompanied me, but nevertheless, a good star stood over my life. I was spared the ultimate grief and my three children could remain with me, all human beings with heart, spirit and soul which live on in the grandchildren and friends. . . . Do not weep and take heart in the fact that I was spared an extended suffering. My life was guided by faith, hope and love, these three, but the greatest of these is love.

✳ ✳ ✳

Moritz and Ida's three children all survived and went off in varied directions to lead very different lives. I knew Susy as a great extrovert with friends all over the world, able to be relaxed and at home wherever she was. My father was far more reserved and happiest at home in New Jersey. Lore was permanently anxious and never fully at home anywhere. They wrote letters to one another, and Susy visited when she passed through New York on the way from South America to Europe, but their ties were strained by the distances of an international diaspora and by my father's fierce secrecy.

STUMBLING STONES

There was one last walk in Hamburg that I needed to take before heading home. I was looking for a flash of sun-struck brass at my feet, a set of *Stolpersteines*, or "stumbling stones." *Stolpersteines* are usually cobblestones set slightly higher than the ones around them, causing an inattentive person to stumble. The stones I sought are the brainchild of artist Gunter Demnig, who intends a different kind of disruption. Demnig, born in 1947, grew up in Berlin, and whenever he asked his parents about Jews, they changed the subject. This had always disturbed him, but in 1996 he came up with an idea of something he could do.

In his garage studio, Demnig creates brass plaques mounted over four-by-four pieces of concrete that can be set into sidewalks like cobblestones. The stones are embedded in front of the addresses where Jews were taken away. Each inscription begins, "Hier wohnte," "Here lived," followed by a name and date of birth, date of seizure, concentration camp and date of death, depending on how much is known. Demnig explains: "I wanted to bring back the names of the Jews who lived, loved, had children and a normal life, who lived in these houses." And he wants to provoke a moment of mental stumbling, of sudden, compelled attention.

I was searching for a cluster of *Stolpersteines* memorializing Edgar, Anna, Karl-Heinz, Richard, and Walter Neumark. I found their names on my family tree and discovered that a case study was done about them to exemplify the Nazis' "euthanasia" of those labeled as defective and living "lives unworthy of life." Edgar grew up in Wittmund, married Anna, and moved to Hamburg where they had three sons. All but Anna were hospitalized and sterilized for being mentally unfit. Walter and Richard were also accused of homosexual acts. Walter was deported and shot in the Izvica Ghetto. Edgar and his other sons were gassed in Brandenburg. Anna was murdered in Minsk.

I spent the night with a German family who attended Trinity's Wee Worship service before they moved back to Hamburg. Their apartment was only a few blocks from Grindallee, and they thought it would be a short walk to the Neumark *Stolpersteines* on that same street, but it turned out to be miles. After walking for a few hours, I was finally nearing my destination, but I could see that the sidewalk ahead of me was torn up. Did I come all this way for nothing? Had the memorial been removed? I came to the address, and there, less than two feet from the end of the construction area, I found the stones. They were covered with a thick layer of dust, so I bought a bottle of water at a nearby bakery. As I bent over the stones, I remembered Gunter Demnig's words: "In order to read the names of the victims, we have to bow down before them." I knelt on the sidewalk and poured a stream of water onto the stones, washing away the dirt, a libation anointing their names—*Edgar, Anna, Karl-Heinz, Richard, Walter*—and sealing them into my heart.

AFTERWORD: PASSOVER IN THE PROMISED LAND

I do a lot of my writing in my office at church because there is no room in our home. Actually, it is almost in my home because the parsonage is attached to the church, and my office is downstairs from our kitchen. The office has a window onto a very busy West 100th Street. We're next to a public-health center and a library and across the street from a playground, a police precinct, and a fire station. We're also on the way to Central Park. I'm usually able to block out the noise, but the window makes it impossible to pretend I'm not here. If people see me inside, they'll knock on the glass to get my attention. I knew this would be a problem when I took off a few months to write, and so I had a blind installed. It works perfectly, which also means that it blocks out all natural light. When the blind is down, my husband refers to the space as my cave, as in, "Are you going into your cave to write now?" or "It's time to come out of that cave to eat dinner!" I don't particularly love writing in a cave. I'd prefer the cabin in the woods or the porch overlooking the lake or the abbey in the desert or basically anywhere else far from peeping parishioners and sirens, but you can't beat the cave for convenience. It's so easy to just pop downstairs and pull the blind with a nod of sympathy to the plants turned ever hopefully toward an abruptly disappearing sun. In the end, all I need is to be left alone with a chair and a laptop.

Sometimes, though, it's gotten very depressing in the cave. I remember one day when it occurred to me that it would be interesting to see if I could find out what happened to my grandfather's siblings and their children. I knew that Bernhard had settled in England, and I had plans to visit his great-granddaughter and her family. I'd also heard of my father's most renowned cousin, Fritz Neumark, a professor of economics who escaped to Turkey and basically transformed the Turkish economy before returning to teach in Germany after the war. Fritz was also a baptized Protestant and died in 1991. Fritz had two children—Matthias who recently died and Veronica who lives in an assisted living facility in Pennsylvania. Gregorio and I visited her, and she told us all about growing up in Istanbul.

I found nothing about Moritz's two sisters, but most of what I did find brought deeper shadows into my cave. Moritz's brother, Max, a concert pianist, was deported to Theresienstadt on the same train as my grandparents. I can find no further record of Max. Abraham Adolf died of natural causes, but his son, Richard, was deported to Theresienstadt along with his wife. They were selected for a train out of the camp five days before Moritz, Ida, and Max arrived. Richard and his wife, Joanna, were murdered at Auschwitz. To secure the safety of their son Hans, they had sent him to a home for Jewish children in Rotterdam. The home was bombed in 1940, and the children were moved to Arnhem. In December 1942, all of the children were taken to Westerbork and then to their deaths at Auschwitz in 1943. A second son, Ernst, was murdered by the Nazis in Dresden.

Julius died at Theresienstadt shortly before Moritz's transport arrived. His son Paul perished at Auschwitz. His son Kurt was deported with his wife, Paula, to Izbeca in Poland, where they were murdered. His son Willi married an Austrian woman who kept the Nazis from taking their only child, Claus Dieter, by denying that Willi was his father. Claus Dieter favored his mother, with blond hair and blue eyes. Willi, a pastry chef, was arrested in 1938, taken to a prison in Berlin and transferred to a Jewish hospital, where he died the following day. He had been poisoned. Claus Dieter was eventually deported to the Mauthausen concentration camp, but he survived to be liberated by the U.S. Army. The records show that he had been arrested under the category of political prisoner, not as a Jew.

I sat deep in the shadows of loss, dazed and sad. I had no energy for the long climb up the stairs back into our kitchen, leaving Germany in the 1930s and 40s and entering into twenty-first–century New York. These people were family, my father's uncles, cousins and their children whom he had never mentioned. I don't know if he had ever known most of them. I made these discoveries on the same day, using various Shoah databases. The search button had become an ominous portal that I approached with increasing trepidation. And then something wonderful happened!

I found a page of testimony about Julius' son Kurt. Although Kurt and his wife were murdered, the form had been filled out by their surviving daughter, Edith Tenn, at the Martyrs Memorial and Museum of the Holocaust in Los Angeles. She had left the testimony in 1987. A little math led me to think it was unlikely that Edith was still alive, but I Googled her name and the home address she'd included on the form in South Gate, California. I was rewarded with a link to a site that told me Edith had died in 1993 at the age of seventy-four. Perhaps she had children? Now I was on a hunt for the living.

I went to *Ancestry.com* and found that Edith Ilse Neumark arrived in California on a boat from Germany in 1939 with her husband, Solomon Tenenbaum, a surname that transitioned into Tenn. I was unable to find any birth records or obituaries that might have named children, but I did find a page from the California voting registry that had a Joe Tenn living near Edith and Solomon. I also found a Ben Tenn. I Googled them and found a website listing a Tenn consulting business run by Ben. I called the phone number and got a recording. "This may sound strange," I began, and asked if Edith was his mother and told him that if so, we were related because his great-grandfather Julius was my grandfather's brother. Within minutes, Ben called back, followed by Joe, and we began the first of many conversations by phone and email about our entwined family history. Suddenly, my cave was beaming with sunshine from California. Although their original family name became less Jewish, they did not. As lifelong, practicing Jews descended from Jews, they were somewhat shocked to learn that they had a Lutheran pastor for a cousin, even a second cousin once removed. So when was I going to visit? The shadows of the dead had delivered me into the warm arms of the living. I ran upstairs to tell my family.

* * *

Thanks to a lovestruck matzah salesman, I ended up boarding a plane to welcome the Sabbath and celebrate the Passover with my Jewish family in California. Solomon Tennenbaum (who went by Sol) was orphaned when he was fourteen years old, and he supported himself by a variety of odd jobs, including taking and delivering matzah orders at Passover. In the spring of 1937, as Sol was going through a suburb of Essen, Germany, taking the orders, he came to the comfortable apartment of my father's cousin, Kurt Neumark, and his wife, Paula. Kurt was a prosperous tobacco salesman, and Paula had opened a hat shop on the ground floor of their building. The couple had three children, including seventeen-year-old Edith, who answered the door when Sol came calling.

The two young people were quickly smitten with each other, much to the displeasure of Edith's parents, who did not view Sol as a proper match for their daughter. Not only was he basically penniless, but he was also one of the *Ostjuden*, eastern Jews with Polish roots, looked down upon by upper-class Germans. Nevertheless, Edith and Sol began to date. There is a sweet snapshot of Sol lifting a laughing Edith in his arms. Both are wearing bathing suits, and it appears as though he is about to drop her into a body of water that is just out of view. It was the summer of 1938.

That fall, *Kristallnacht* devastated their romantic idyll. Edith's mother's hat shop was wrecked, the Neumark home was badly damaged, and her father was arrested and taken to the Dachau concentration camp. Since Sol was not German and had lost his Polish citizenship when his father died, he was officially stateless and was not arrested at that time. He soon proposed to Edith. Under any other circumstances, it is doubtful that her parents would have given their permission, but Sol had a card up his sleeve, literally. His uncle, William, and older brother, Joe, had gone to live in California and could sponsor Sol and Edith for visas if the marriage was allowed. By that point, their daughter's survival was more important to her parents than class differences.

Amazingly, Edith's mother, Paula, was able to get Kurt out of Dachau by showing officials the Iron Cross he received for heroism in World War I. Kurt signed the paperwork required to approve the marriage, and Sol and Edith became husband and wife in January 1939 in front of a Nazi official who kept a cigar in his mouth the entire time, spitting out the words. Edith was nineteen years old and Sol was twenty-five. In March, they left on a freighter that took them through the Panama Canal to Los Angeles, where Uncle William and Joe awaited them.

∗ ∗ ∗

Edith and Sol's youngest son, Ben, met me at the airport in his white Acura and drove me through the San Fernando Valley to the spacious home that he shares with his wife, Cindy, who welcomed us with a wide smile and a warm hug. While she finished preparing our Sabbath meal, Ben gave me a tour of their house and took me out to their pool area surrounded by palm and grapefruit trees and a cactus garden. He showed me the spot where a cactus plant purchased by Edith in Panama for thirty-five cents had spent the last portion of its seventy years. Edith and Sol were each allowed to take only five dollars out of Germany, and they bought almost nothing on their voyage except for the cactus—a birthday gift for Edith who turned twenty during the trip. She and Sol would soon celebrate the birth of their first child, Joseph, followed by Miriam, Daniel and Ben.

Ben and I went inside as the clouds flushed pink, and I sat at the table for what was going to be my very first *Shabbat*. I had read Abraham Heschel's beautiful book on the Sabbath in college. He writes of the Sabbath as "a sanctuary in time," as we labor among the ruins of this world, the Sabbath gives us a glimpse of the world as it should be, a vision, and even a momentary experience, of Jerusalem as the city of shalom. There are some parallels between the Jewish Sabbath and Christian worship, but each is also unique, and I have longed to sit at this Sabbath table. Cindy lit the candles and said a blessing. We ate a delicious meal of lemon chicken and potatoes and shared countless family stories. We were eating at the kitchen table set beside glass doors leading out to the pool area. Through the glass, you could see the lights of a distant city, shimmering against the dark sky like Sabbath jewels.

The next day, the intense preparations for the Passover seder began. This was the first time I was a behind-the-scenes Passover participant. As other cousins rolled in from around the state, I helped stuff deviled eggs and set the table with Wedgewood china and silver. Before long, all fifteen guests arrived. The meal we would enjoy was ready: deviled eggs and gefilte fish, matzah ball soup, lamb from a recipe in Edith's 1938 cookbook, vegetables, and kugel. A family friend brought cookies for dessert and Cindy had prepared her delicious butter brickle with broken up pieces of matzah, butter, brown sugar, chocolate bits, and pecans. Before the main meal, we shared the symbolic foods of Passover—the bread of affliction, the sweet mortar and bitter herbs, the spring greens dipped in salt-water tears.

Ben sat at the head of the table and led us through the *Haggadah*. It was the first time that their five-year old granddaughter was old enough to ask the questions meant for children. They begin, "Why is this night different from all other nights?" Ben offered the traditional answers, recalling the Exodus story of slavery and freedom, but for me there were other answers as well. This night was different because I could now see my own family's oppression and journey to liberation through the lens of the Exodus story. Now, with the cry of the enslaved Israelites, I heard the distant weeping and groans of my own relatives, my grandparents, and my father.

Although my Moses, my grandfather, did not survive to be liberated, he left a trail for me to follow. Were it not so, there would have been no Wikipedia page for my daughter to approach and, at the touch of a keyboard, part the sea of oblivion, opening a path for me on another night unlike any other that led me to this table, lifting my glass and speaking Hebrew blessings in the candlelight. We sat together to share this Passover meal because of an exodus just one generation removed. We were in the promised land of southern California, and yet I find myself unsettled still, in a wilderness that defies resolution.

At the table, we are singing *Dayenu*, getting louder and louder with each verse: "If God had brought us out of Egypt—*Dayenu!* . . . If God had split the sea for us—*Dayenu!* . . . If God had fed us manna—*Dayenu!* . . . If God had given us Shabbat—*Dayenu!* . . . If God had given us the Torah—*Dayenu!*" *Dayenu* means "it would have been enough." I have my own questions about what is enough. Have I done enough to bear testimony to my Jewish forebears? What more can and should I do?

When I was in seminary, over thirty years ago, I was responsible for planning some community chapel services including one in November. It fell on *Kristallnacht*, This was not a date I recall anyone ever mentioning at the school, but I was aware of it. I remember walking down a street near campus and noticing an old window lying against a garbage can. I brought it back, found a hammer, and broke it into pieces that I scattered all over the altar. I don't recall any details of the liturgy of remembrance and repentance that I created, but I do remember the reactions. Some people expressed their appreciation and quite a few were dismayed and angry about splintered glass on the altar. I didn't know then that I was reenacting a desecration central to my own history, my own shattered legacy. I didn't know how deep that glass would cut. Now I also see my call to places ravaged by injustice and people targeted by others' prejudice and hate through the lens of that same broken glass.

I am also beginning to see how this history and its jagged edges have worked its way into the lives of my own children without my knowing it. Our daughter, Ana, whose Google search set this journey in motion, is highly sensitive to nonverbal cues, which is why she is so amazing in her work with young children on the autistic spectrum. She calls with excitement to tell me whenever a child in her classroom speaks their first word. I realize now what should have been evident immediately—it is not surprising that Ana is the one who unlocked our family silence. And perhaps, too, she was unconsciously led to her own vocation because of our family history, stuck without speech or any expressed emotional connection to this buried past for so many years. Only time will tell how the impact of this story will continue to move through my children and any generations to come. Its power to shape our lives, seemingly without our will, is both wondrous and unsettling.

* * *

Although I long to have known my grandfather, to have heard his voice and felt his warmth, he is so much more to me now than a specter in an old photograph, and I love him in ways that were impossible before. Although I yearn to speak with my Oma now, as an adult, she has emerged from my past as a heroine and mentor of resilience for the later years of life. My heart remains full of questions my father is not here to answer, yet I feel closer to him than ever, no longer needing to guess at the source of sorrow pooled in his eyes. I wonder what he thinks to see me at this Passover table, though if he sees me here, it is through eyes washed clear of earthly shadows. I think they would all approve of my plan to study German, although when this book is finished, I'm first going back to the Hebrew I loved in seminary and forgot in the Bronx when Spanish took over the language learning center of my brain. Hebrew letters have been dancing in my dreams.

From a history of horror, I have received staggering gifts of truth, identity, and love. This is something we all long for and need, and we can help to make it happen, one story at a time. Listening without prejudice or pity to those who are willing to recount their narratives of pain, loss, and righteous rage is part of changing the world. Another challenge is recognizing and naming our complicity in such narratives. Those of us who belong to religious communities can join to dismantle the architecture of judgment with all of its closets and shadowy corners and resurrect our history of sanctuary—not only for those fleeing violence and poverty in other lands but for refugees closer to home seeking community where they can be their authentic selves. We cannot undo the past, but there remains plenty that calls for our outcry and action today. What we do will vary, but I pray that we will not do nothing.

Exploring our family trees is an exciting and precarious venture. Even if you lose your balance, as I surely did, you can land in a new place where you always belonged. If I had only learned a portion of what has been revealed and recovered, it would have been more than I imagined possible. I am blessed by all my once-lost kin, those at this Passover table and those who people my heart, whose memory has enlarged the twin chambers of my being . . . and I look forward to those to come. In the course of writing this book, I have become the proud mother-in-law to my daughter's very Jewish wife who may, God-willing, give me Jewish grandchildren. So perhaps I will dance at their bat mitzvah or bar mitzvah—the one my father never had. I will always long to know more, to do more, to write more and yet, this night, these gifts suffice. *Dayenu. Dayenu. Dayenu.*

ACKNOWLEDGMENTS

My mind spins to think of all the many people across the globe to whom I owe a debt of gratitude. Posthumously, there is Edzard Eichenbaum whom I was fortunate to meet and become the beneficiary of his prodigious research on the Jews of Wittmund, among them my ancestors. There is Carsten Burfeind who selflessly gave of his vacation time to be my translator in Wittmund and who assisted my research and served as my guide in Berlin. I am thankful for my cousin Klaus and Tante Renate who were willing to shed light on family secrets, uncomfortable as it was.

In Lübeck, I owe thanks to Dr. Ingeburgh Klatt, director of the Burgkloster Museum, who organized key visits, chauffeured me, assisted me and fed me, and to Pastor Egbert Staabs who welcomed me and my son to the museum he helped to establish about my grandfather's work. Dr. Bernd Schwarze kindly made time to give me a private tour of St. Mary's chancel with the font. On my second trip to Lübeck, I enjoyed the lavish hospitality of Pastor Ina Brinkmann and her husband Jacob. Ina also helped to initiate meetings with Mayor Bernd Saxe, city archivist Dr. Jan Lokers, and a group of young theologians dedicated to researching the painful history of the church and the Jews of Lübeck. I am grateful to them all.

In England, my newly discovered second cousin Lesley Hayward and her husband Ted welcomed my family into their home as we shared our genealogical research and discoveries. I experienced the same attentive welcome and passion for family history in California with more newly discovered cousins, Joe and Ben Tenn and Ben's wife, Cindy. My extended family in Australia (Barbara, Peter, Katherine) cheered me on as well and shared what they knew.

In Poland, I am thankful for Piotr Hnatyszyn, director of the City Museum in Zabrze, who with his wife arranged visits and escorted me and my husband around the area where my grandmother grew up and met and married my grandfather.

Closer to home I am thankful for conversations with several psychotherapists and authors—Dr. Eugene Pogany with his own family legacy of suffering in the Shoah and Dr. Eva Fogelman, a world-renowned expert in the generational impact of trauma from the Shoah. Dr. Fogelman encouraged me to shift from historical investigation to exploring related psychological terrain. Additionally, I am thankful to Dr. Judy Roth whose work is influenced by her own family's Shoah history. She was a generous reader of my manuscript, and like the others, she asked probing questions that jogged my memory and led me to appreciate the power of unconscious communication from one generation to another.

My writing has benefited from many thoughtful, kind, and critically astute readers. I am particularly grateful to Helen Atsma, Christina Del Piero, Lydie Raschka, Lisa Horowitz, and two neighboring rabbis, Jeremy Kalmanofsky and Roland Matalon, who offered their gracious support and encouragement on my literary and spiritual journey.

I am humbled and thankful for Inge Auerbacher's visit to me. Her story of survival at Theresienstadt shed light on my grandparents' own experiences. I am most grateful for the gracious, informative attention I received from two giants of German Jewish history: Dr. Ismar Schorsch, the chancellor-emeritus of the Jewish Theological Seminary in Manhattan, and Dr. Frank Mecklenburg, Director of Research and Chief Archivist at the Leo Baeck Institute here in New York. While many email inquiries end up deleted by busy scholars, I am thankful that this was not true when I wrote to Marion Kaplan, Professor of Hebrew and Judaic Studies at Columbia University. In addition to her own writings, she provided me with an exceptionally helpful list of research ideas.

A book project requires significant time and, in this case, travel. This would have been impossible for me without the generous support of the Louisville Institute that funded a good part of my international travel and the Collegeville Institute that provided time apart for reflection and writing. Thanks to Don Ottenhoff for his enduring faith in this project and to Carla Durand for her logistical magic. I am also a grateful beneficiary of a Trexler study and travel grant through the Metropolitan New York Synod of the ELCA.

On the publishing end, I'm thankful to my agent John Thornton who is always more than just an agent, going above and beyond with editorial precision and providing unflagging hope in the face of mounting rejections. I am thankful to Debra Bendis at *The Christian Century* for publishing some early essays and to Richard Kauffman for introducing me to Lil Copan when she was at Abingdon and for her willingness to take on this book and to put it in the hands of Lauren Winner for a daunting and delightful editing journey. A big thank you to the whole team at Abingdon especially Ramona Richards,

Cat Hoort, and Brenda Smotherman for working hard to send this story out into the world, far and wide.

I am indebted to the people of Trinity Lutheran Church of Manhattan for the many and varied ways they encourage and support my vocation as pastor and writer and for their eagerness to live towards radical hospitality and prophetic zeal. I am thankful to my Trinity Place Shelter colleagues, especially Kevin and Wendy, fierce, tireless collaborators in the grit and grace of life-saving work.

First and finally, I am thankful for my family—my parents and the cloud of witnesses gone before me who I hope to honor here. May their memory be for a blessing. And for my immediate family—Ana who set the whole journey in motion and Hans, my intrepid travel companion—this story is flesh of your flesh too. . . . and to Gregorio who has been an enthusiastic, patient partner through it all . . . love and thanksgiving beyond words.

Soli Deo Gloria

Endnotes

Preface: Googling Moses
" . . . the shadows of time" Nelly Sachs, *O The Chimneys: Selected Poems*
(Farrar, Straus and Giroux: New York, 1969), 43.

"Theresienstadt (Terezin)" Throughout the book, I have chosen to use the
German name for the camp since my German grandparents would have
likely used the German name.

1. CROSSING OVER

My German Trousseau
"after 1935, it was illegal . . ." Throughout the book, there are references
to key people, events and dates from the era of the Third Reich. This
historical information comes from the following works:

Amos Elon, *The Pity of It All: A Portrait of the German-Jewish Epoch,
1743–1933* (Picador: New York, 2003).

Saul Friedländer, *Nazi Germany and the Jews 1933–1945* (Harper
Perennial: New York, 2009).

Marion Kaplan, *Jewish Daily Life in Germany 1618–1945* (Oxford
University Press: New York, 2005).

Marion Kaplan: *Between Dignity and Despair: Jewish Life in Nazi Germany*
(Oxford University Press: New York, 1998).

Michael A. Meyer, editor: *German-Jewish History in Modern Times*

> *Volume 1 Tradition and Enlightenment 1600–1780*

> *Volume 2 Emancipation and Acculturation 1780–1871*

> *Volume 3 Integration in Dispute 1871–1918*

> *Volume 4 Renewal and Destruction 1918–1945*

(Columbia University Press, New York, 1998).

A Boy That Wept
"And she opened it, and saw . . . a boy that wept." Martin Buber, *Tales of the Hasidim: Later Masters* (Schocken Books: New York, 1948), 301-302.

"A strange lostness . . ." Paul Celán, *Poems of Paul Celán* (Persea Books: New York, 1972), 149.

2. WITTMUND

Edzard's Big Hobby
Herbert Reyer and Martin Tielke, *The History of Jews in Wittmund.*

"Daten Zur Geschkichte der Juden in Wittmud Und die Wittmunder Judenfamilien Neumark" (Frisia Judaica Verlag Ostfriesische Landschaft: Aurich, 1988).

"the mobs tore up feather blankets and pillows . . ." Kaplan, *Between Dignity and Despair,* 125.

"Rabbi Jacob Emden . . ."Megilat Sefer The Autobiography of Rabbi Jacob Emden (1697–1776) translated by Rabbi Leperer and Rabbi Wise (Publishyoursefer.com: Baltimore, MD, 2011).

Re-membering
"refugees from Brandenburg in 1510 . . ." (http://www.jewishvirtuallibrary.org/jsource/judaica/ejud_0002_0004_0_03436.html)

"Dietrich Bonhoeffer . . . in his book Ethics" Dietrich Bonhoeffer, *Dietrich Bonhoeffer Works, Volume 6, Ethics* (Fortress Press: Minneapolis, MN, 2009).

"a spiritual existence that takes no part . . ." Ibid., 57.

"We are otherworldly . . ." Dietrich Bonhoeffer, *Dietrich Bonhoeffer Works, Volume 12, Berlin:1932–1933* (Fortress Press: Minneapolis, MN, 2009), 286.

"He spoke of being one cake . . . common and one . . ." Martin Luther, *"'All Become One Cake' A Sermon on the Lord's Supper,"* Maundy Thursday, 1523 (LCMS World Relief and Human Care: St. Louis, Missouri, 2005), 3.

"I give myself for the common good . . ." Ibid., 3.

"There are those indeed who would gladly share . . ." Martin Luther, *Luther's Works: Word and Sacrament, Volume 35* (Fortress Press: Philadelphia,1960), 57.

"They are unwilling . . . ." Ibid., 57.

"Of the Jews and Their Lies," Martin Luther, *Luther's Works, Volume 47: "The Christian in Society" IV* (Philadelphia: Fortress Press, 1971), 268-293.

ELCA Formal Declaration to the Jewish Community (http://www.elca. org/en/Faith/Ecumenical-and-Inter-Religious-Relations/Inter-Religious-Relations/Jewish-Relations).

A Meeting Place for the Sages
"Let your house be . . ." The Living Talmud: The Wisdom of the Fathers (The Heritage Press: New York, 1955), 9.

"He brought out a copy . . ." What follows is the full text of the S.S. report:

> The action against the Jews in the District of Wittmund happened without any particular incident. Of the three still remaining Jewish retail stores, two were damaged and one only somewhat.
>
> All Jewish people were kept by the S.A. in protective custody. However, women and children were released in the early morning hours. As originally commanded, the Jewish men were deported to Oldenburg by group transportation.
>
> All cash secured by the S.A. during the action remains in se-cure custody with the local S.A. Administration. In the same way,

the complete inventory of the Jewish retail stores was secured by the N.S.V. The exact amount of cash and the quantities of merchandise are not known to this office.

The burning of the synagogue (in the nearby town) created some problems, since the synagogue is located in the old part of town and is closely surrounded by old buildings. Under supervision of the Fire Brigade, the surrounding buildings could be protected and damage avoided.

The Jewish-owned "Horster Grashaus " agricultural enterprise was put under the guardianship of the District Farm Director in order to secure orderly, uninterrupted continuation of the activities.

3. LÜBECK

The Iron Works

"A book produced . . ." Lübecker Industriekultur: Leben und Arbeit in Herrenwyk: Geschichte der Hochofenwerk Lúbeck (AG, der Werkskolonie und ihrer Menschen, 1985), 23.

The Font and the Pit

"Once a hole opens . . ." Ursula Hegi, *Children and Fire* (Scribner: New York, 2011), 93.

"Between 1880 and 1919 in Germany . . ." Michael A. Meyer, editor: *German-Jewish History in Modern Times, Volume 3,* 15-16.

"An Event Without a Witness: Barry Ulanov Memorial Lecture," Union Theological Seminary, New York, May 11, 2011.

"The Murmuring Deep . . ." Avivah Gottlieb Zornberg, *The Murmuring Deep; Reflections on the Biblical Unconscious* (Schocken Books: New York, 2009).

"Joseph and his screams . . ." Ibid., 301.

"Zornberg notes that Joseph . . ." Ibid., 302.

"As Rashi points out . . ." Ibid., 303.

"R. Zodok HaCohen says . . ." Ibid., 309.

"All shall be well . . ." Julian of Norwich, *Revelations of Divine Love* (Methuen & Co.LTD: London, 1958), 57.

"It was so widespread that . . ." Meyer, *Volume 1*, 24.

"Children who have been baptized . . ." *Saving Jewish Children, but at What Cost?* (New York Times, January 9, 2005).

"For children who no longer have their parents . . ." Ibid.

"In 1858, a six-year-old Jewish child . . ." Ibid.

Knit Together
"As the Spanish wretches went about . . ." Bartolomé de las Casas, *The Devastation of the Indies* (Johns Hopkins University Press: Baltimore, 1974), 81.

"One tribal chief was being preached at . . ." Ibid., 45.

Totentanz
"Shortly afterward, the firm was bought . . ." L. M. Stallbaumer, "Big Business and the Persecution of the Jews: The Flick Concern and the 'Aryanization' of Jewish Property Before the War," *Holocaust and Genocide Studies,* 13 (Spring 1999), 1-27.

"After the war, Flick would be convicted . . ." *Law Reports of Trials of War Criminals, Volume IX, The Trial of Frederick Flick* (The United Nations War Crimes Commission, 1949), 1-22.

The Bells of St. Mary's
"When Christ calls a man . . ." Dietrich Bonhoeffer, *The Cost of Discipleship* (MacMillan: New York, 1963), 99.

"It is living, no rather dying, suffering . . ." Martin Luther, *Sämmlische Schriften, Volume 4* (St, Louis: Concordia Publishing House, 1957), 455.

"To celebrate is to invoke God's presence . . ." Abraham J . Heschel, *Who Is Man?* (Stanford University Press: Stanford, 1965), 117.

"Never shall I forget that nocturnal silence . . ." Elie Wiesel, *Night* (Avon Books: New York, 1958), 44.

"Where is God? Where is He?" Ibid., 76.

". . . after two thousand years of 'Christianity' . . ." Marc Chagall, speech in February 1944 quoted at exhibition, *Chagall: Love, War and Exile* at Jewish Museum, New York City.

"Hitler announced that churches . . ." Kyle Jantzen, *Faith and Fatherland: Parish Politics in Hitler's Germany* (Fortress Press: Minneapolis, 2008), 3.

Already in 1933, the baptism . . . Friedländer, 18.

"Just as a pig remains a pig . . ." Susannah Heschel, *The Aryan Jesus: Christian Theologians and the Bible in Nazi Germany* (Princeton University Press: Princeton, 2008), 55.

"In 1934 Bishop Erwin Balzer came to St. Mary's . . ." Albrecht Schreiber, *"Gedenke der Vorigen Zeiten:" Illustrierte Chronik der Juden in Moisling und Lübeck* (Edition Nord: Lübeck, 2009), 35.

"My theological position is derived . . ." Albrecht Schreiber, *Zwischen Hakenkreuz und Holstentor -Lübeck 1925 bis 1939 - von der Krise bis zum Krieg* (Lübecker Nachrichten, 1983), 84.

"Immediately following Kristallnacht, . . ." S. Heschel, 76.

"In the spring of 1939 . . ." Annette Göhres, Stephan Linck, Joachim Liß-Walther, *Als Jesus "arisch" wurde: Kirche, Christen, Juden in Nordelbien 1933–1945,* Die Ausstellung in Kiel (Bremen: Edition Temmen, 2003), 44.

"He also brought on Johannes Sievers . . ." Ibid., 45.

"The Institute's purpose . . ." S. Heschel, 77ff.

"Jesus was Aryanized . . ." Ibid., 58ff.

"Prayers were redirected . . ." Ibid., 11.

"Today Jesus appears to us . . ." Richard Steigmann-Gall, *The Holy Reich: Nazi Conceptions of Christianity, 1919–1945* (Cambridge University Press: Cambridge, 2003), 96.

"Please understand my position against . . ." Annette Göhres, Stephan Linck, Joachim Liß-Walther, 176.

"Although the hearty embrace met . . ." Ibid., 45.

"As a Christian, I also have . . ." S. Heschel, 10.

"Jews cannot be members . . ." Annette Göhres, Stephan Linck, Joachim Liß-Walther, 44.

"As part of the German nation . . ." Ibid., 51.

"Even this did not go far enough . . ." Ibid., 51.

"The Confessing Church concentrated too much . . ." Wolfgang Gerlach, *And the Witnesses Were Silent: The Confessing Church and the Persecution of the Jews* (The University of Nebraska Press, Lincoln, 2000), 232.

"The church's unconditional obligation . . ." Dietrich Bonhoeffer, Ibid., 365.

"not only binding up the wounds . . ." Ibid., 365.

5. BERLIN

A Green Shade

"Annihilating all that's made . . ." Andrew Marvell "The Garden" *(http://www.poetryfoundation.org/poem/173948).*

The Ark

Paperwalls: America and the Refugee Crisis 1938–1941, David S. Wyman (Pantheon Books: New York, 1968).

The Abandonment of the Jews: America and the Holocaust 1941–1945, David S. Wyman (The New Press: New York, 1984).

"Nazi sympathizers held a large rally . . ." Wyman, *Paperwalls*, 15.

"Father Charles Coughlin from . . ." Ibid., 17ff.

"The most anti-Semitic part of the country . . ." Wyman, *The Abandonment of the Jews*, 10.

"President Roosevelt responded immediately . . ." Wyman, *Paperwalls*, 43ff.

"A Newsweek reporter summed it up . . ." Ibid., 50.

"Attorney General Robert Jackson . . ." Ibid., 186.

Glory, Laud and Honor
"Between 1933 and 1939 . . ." Meyer, Volume 4, 231.

"I read that seven thousand Jews . . ." Beate Meyer, Hermann Simon, and Chana Schütz (Eds.), *Jews in Nazi Berlin: From Kristallnacht to Liberation* (University of Chicago Press: Chicago, 2009), 334.

"Prior to their arrest . . ." Ibid., 188

"One Czech survivor recalls . . ." Schiff, 80.

6. THERESIENSTADT

The Fowler's Snare
I Never Saw Another Butterfly: Children's Drawings and Poems from Terezín Concentration Camp 1942–1944, Hana Volavkova (Schocken: New York, 1987).

The historical information about Theresienstadt comes from the following books:

Days of Sorrow and Pain: Leo Baeck and the Berlin Jews, Leonard Baker (Oxford University Press: New York, 1978).

Hitler's Gift: The Story of Theresienstadt, George E. Berkley (Branden Books: Boston, 1993).

Theresienstadt: The Town the Nazis Gave to the Jews, Vera Schiff (Vera Schiff, 1996).

Theresienstadt: Hitler's Gift to the Jews, Norbert Troller (The University of North Carolina Press: Chapel Hill, 1991).

Winter has come, and with it a great chill . . . The Terezín Diary of Gonda Redlich, Saul. S Friedman (Ed.) (University Press of Kentucky: Lexington, 1992), 96.

"According to a nurse . . ." Berkely, 53.

"If Berlin, for example, had had the same population . . ." Berkely, 46.

"sometimes there was lentil soup . . ." Troller, 52-53.

"Unattached and unassisted, they suffered . . ." Schiff, 112-13.

I am a Star: Child of the Holocaust, Inge Auerbacher (Puffin Books: New York, 1993).

"By no means did we sit weeping . . ." Will To Create, Will to Live: The Culture of Terezin, a program of the 92nd Street Y, January 9–February 16, 2012.

"The ever-present threat of deportation . . ." Berkely, 71-72.

"[we] watched anxiously, observing . . ." Gerda Haas.

7. POST-WAR

Reconstruction
"We tacitly embarked on a conspiracy . . ." Schiff, ix.

After Years of Forgetting
"We must always take sides . . ." Elie Wiesel, Nobel Acceptance Speech, 1986.

A Good Star
A Woman in Berlin, Eight Weeks in a Conquered City, Anonymous (Picador: New York, 2000).

Stumbling Stones
"I found their names . . ." (http://www.stolpersteinehamburg.de/?MAIN_ID=7&BIO_ID=319)

AFTERWORD: PASSOVER IN THE PROMISED LAND

"I had read Abraham Heschel's beautiful . . ." Abraham Joshua Heschel, *The Sabbath: Its Meaning for Modern Man* (Farrar, Straus and Giroux: New York, 1951).